The Early America
Furnituremaker's
Manual

"To improve home workshop enthusiasts' knowledge and give them additional ideas . . . Clearly written so that any reasonably experienced woodworker should have no trouble [building] the sixteen pieces the text features."　　　　　　　　—Bernard Gladstone in *The New York Times*

"Useful for students . . . Clearly written."　　　　　　　*—Booklist*

Every aspect of furniture making and finishing is explained, including:
- Woods — their characteristics and why each is chosen for a particular purpose
- Glues — hot, cold, and contact — ready mix and dry powder
- Sandpaper — sizes, types, and techniques to use
- Dovetailing
- Wood finishing — materials and procedures; stain mixtures

The step-by-step directions are explicit, easy to follow, and fully illustrated with photographs and working drawings. There are also tips on how the basic designs can be varied in size and shape, and on how different pieces can be used in many ways throughout the house.

A. W. Marlow, with fifty-two years of experience, is a master craftsman who reproduces period furniture pieces in his shop in York, Pennsylvania. A contributor to *Fine Woodworking* Magazine, he is the author of four other books.

BOOKS BY A.W. MARLOW

Fine Furniture for the Amateur Cabinetmaker
The Cabinetmaker's Treasury (with F. E. Hoard)
Available in paperback as
Good Furniture You Can Make Yourself
The Early American Furnituremaker's Manual
Classic Furniture Projects

The Early American Furnituremaker's Manual

The Early American Furniture-maker's Manual

A. W. MARLOW

A SCARBOROUGH BOOK
STEIN AND DAY/*Publishers*/New York

FIRST SCARBOROUGH BOOKS EDITION 1983

The Early American Furnituremaker's Manual was originally published in hardcover
by Macmillan Publishing Co., Inc., and is reprinted by arrangement.
Copyright © 1973 by A.W. Marlow
All rights reserved.
Printed in the United States of America
Stein and Day/*Publishers*
Scarborough House
Briarcliff Manor, N.Y. 10510

Library of Congress Cataloging in Publication Data

Marlow, A.W. (Andrew W.)
    The early American furnituremaker's manual.

    Reprint.   Originally published: New York:
Macmillan, 1973.
    1. Furniture making — Amateurs' manuals.   2. Furni-
ture, Early American — United States.   I. Title.
TT195.M36   1983   684.1′04′0973   83-375
ISBN 0-8128-6184-1 (pbk.)

FOREWORD

Here is a book to fill the need of every home workshop enthusiast who feels the urge to make some Early American furniture for his home. It is written particularly for the hobbyist who wants to learn just enough about furniture construction, materials to use, and simple finishing methods so he can turn out good-looking pieces for his home.

The great number of hobbyists with these aspirations are not interested in the intricacies of design originated by Chippendale, Hepplewhite, or Sheraton. Their goal is to build popular American furniture which they will be proud to use and show in their homes. Always keeping this point of view in mind, we have selected only the pieces in which the highest degree of interest has been shown.

To construct the pieces herein illustrated you will need only the basic machine tools found in nearly every home workshop, i.e., circular saw, small band saw, lathe, and jointer. Occasionally the use of a jigsaw would help perform certain operations with much greater ease than to rely on a hand scroll saw. Add to these machine tools a reasonably good selection of hand tools and your shop is sufficiently equipped to make this desirable furniture.

An attractive feature that will appeal to readers is the fact that all materials, including hardware, may be purchased locally. No letter-writing for catalogues, no delays, no purchases to be made unseen.

CONTENTS

The Early American Furnituremaker's Manual

º1º

General Information

For those having little experience in elementary woodworking, a few hints on what to expect of the various cabinet woods, glues, sanding procedures, etc. will be quite helpful.

WOODS: THEIR CHARACTERISTICS AND WHY EACH IS CHOSEN FOR A GIVEN PURPOSE

White pine, either knotty or clear, is popular with the home woodworker. It is readily available even in less populated areas. Much pine furniture was made in early America because of its workability with hand tools, enduring qualities, and close source of supply. Its use, however, is not recommended for certain structural parts because of its softness. To name a few of the more important parts where a harder wood is desirable, we can start with turnings of all kinds, especially chair-leg turnings. Three-quarter-inch thick drop-leaf tabletops and leaves require a harder wood because hinge screws cannot be sufficiently long to assure permanent holding properties.

Other structural parts that should employ a firmer wood are large drawer sides and backs for two reasons: the bottom edges of drawer sides will wear quickly if made of pine, and cutting dovetails in this spongy wood is much more difficult than a wood with the firmness of poplar. As a seeming contradiction, we do feature drawer dovetailing in pieces made entirely of pine for two reasons. First, even made of soft pine, a dovetailed drawer is much stronger and more rigid than one employing other joining methods. Second, since pine must be used for the drawer front (which will have the tails cut into the ends) the side pieces may as well be of pine also. It will be observed, however, that where this situation exists, a special dovetail pattern with wider tails is recommended. Also, plank-bottom chair seats made of pine will not hold the legs firm for long because the wood around the legs will crush easily, allowing the legs to wobble—progressively making the holes larger and larger.

A final word concerning pine: Because of its popularity, we will, wherever we can find original examples, combine pine with a harder wood. Combination of woods in a single piece of furniture is not at all rare.

Hard maple. Hard is emphasized because soft maple cannot be worked any more easily than the hard variety. Furthermore, the soft wood will neither sand nearly as well nor take as good a finish as the hard.

Early American maple furniture was generally made without too many decorative features. Its hard, dense texture makes it one of the most difficult native woods to work with hand tools.

Curly maple or, what would be even more desirable, striped tiger maple is usually preferred over straight-grained wood because of its decorative qualities. Straight-grained hard maple is generally available at the retail level in necessary thickness.

Cherry or fruitwood is excellent for cabinetmaking. The demand for furniture made of cherry has increased tremendously in the last decade. It has more natural color than maple and this tends to increase the feeling of warmth when finished. Compared to maple in other respects, it is equally durable, it can be worked better with hand tools, and comparable time spent sanding results in a more satisfactory job.

There is only one reason, in our judgment, for choosing maple in preference to cherry for a particular piece to be made; that choice is figure conformation or tiger stripe if available. Rarely can one find much figure in cherry. Cherry lumber may be harder to procure in some areas of the country than maple.

Walnut is a hard, open-grained wood and one of the most desirable native woods for cabinetmaking. In early America walnut was so plentiful that much prime wood was wasted in making anything and everything. The home-workshop enthusiast will find that working with walnut is a gratifying experience. It is a hard wood but, because of its open pores, it can be worked easily with hand tools. An added attraction is the dark color of walnut. It is an interesting wood for the hobbyist because little or no stain is needed when finishing. There may be a few areas where walnut is not stocked by dealers but, in general, it is obtainable without difficulty.

Poplar is a wood rarely used for case work. Its quality of firmness and the ease with which it can be worked indicate its normal uses: drawer sides, backs, bottoms; drawer division frames (except the exterior front piece); and any other interior construction parts. The exception to this concealment rule is the use of poplar for solid-wood chair and settee seats.

Hickory. The furniture described and illustrated in this book suggests the use of hickory for one purpose only—chair-back spindles. White oak may be substituted, if necessary.

Other native woods such as the Oak family, Ash, Elm, and Gum have not shown enough popularity to warrant consideration.

GLUES: HOT, COLD, AND CONTACT—
READY MIX AND DRY POWDER

Hide glue was the only bonding agent used until the twentieth century. Present-day hide glue comes granulated for quick dissolution in hot water.

Older forms were sheets or sticks that had to be dissolved in cold water overnight before heating for use. We of the older school find many traditional methods still satisfactory—including, with few exceptions, hot glue, even though an electric glue pot is a necessary piece of equipment. The chief characteristic of hot glue is its quick-setting feature. Exceptions to the use of hot glue are any situations where large surfaces must be coated, requiring more time than is allowable before clamping.

The foregoing is simply an explanation of normal practice in our shop. The average hobbyist will probably find one of the new adhesives much more convenient for the few occasions when a bonding agent is needed.

Hide glue may be purchased also in ready-mix form. It is packaged in a can and should be used cold without any further preparation. It is much slower setting than the hot variety.

Casein is a dry powder to be mixed with cold water. The occasions when we need a slow-setting glue, casein is preferred in our shop. It has what some potential users would consider a fault—it will stain woods like cherry and walnut; but we overlook this in favor of its other qualities. Casein is an adhesive that must be mixed each day, as it cannot be held over from one day to the next.

There are other brands of both ready mix and powders with qualifications we do not question. Our object here is to pass on to the hobbyist what, we know from experience, he can expect of the materials discussed.

Contact cement is one of the newer adhesives and does not need clamp pressure for bonding. Since we are not familiar with this product, we will forego comment.

SANDPAPER

Quality in this product is as important as the whole operation of sanding. The use of "flint" papers will dishearten every hobbyist who tries them. Find the supplier in your locality who handles good "garnet" cabinet and finishing papers.

Two grit numbers of garnet paper are necessary for cabinet work. Saw marks and planer "waves" can be removed best with coarse 1/2 paper. Follow up with finer 3/0. Your garnet-paper supplier will probably have two types of 3/0 paper. One is called "cabinet" and the other "finishing." Cabinet paper is heavier and less pliable; also it is close coated, which means the cutting particles are bonded to the paper in a much closer formation. Finishing makes use of thin, tough, pliable paper and is open coated, meaning fewer cutting particles are bonded to the paper per square inch. In our shop the choice is 3/0 finishing paper.

Sanding suggestions. Thorough sanding for consistently good finishes must be stressed to the limit. Whenever a hobbyist is discouraged with his finished product, the fault can usually be traced to insufficient sanding.

Sandpaper sheets are of a standard size, 9″ × 11″. To get a convenient working-size piece, crease a full sheet in half and tear; crease a half sheet in the middle and tear to get two quarter-size sheets, 4 1/2″ × 5 1/2″.

For flat work, make a "sanding block" of soft wood or sheet cork (preferably cork) 3″ × 4″ × 7/8″. Center the block on a quarter-size sheet and fold the paper around it. Hand-grip the block and paper as a unit for use.

Until experience teaches you how much sanding is necessary, work by this rule: Start with 1/2 paper, sand until all saw or planer marks appear to be sanded out, then sand again about the same length of time. Always sand with the grain, especially when working with coarse paper.

The most successful method for handsanding a large surface (for example, a tabletop) is to start at a near corner. Develop a natural, easy stroke, which may be 12 to 15 inches in length. While continuing this back-and-forth motion, gradually move the block completely across the tabletop surface; then, just as slowly, return to the starting point. If your natural stroke is about 14 inches, the next pass across and return should advance up the table top about 7 inches. Continue until the entire top has been worked. Use the same procedure and length of working time with 3/0 paper. This should produce an acceptable surface for a good finish.

As construction progresses, bear in mind that each member piece can be sanded much more easily before obstructions are added at the ends or sides. Tabletop edges should be sanded before the top is attached to the table. The top surface may be sanded after attachment.

WOOD FINISHING:
MATERIALS AND PROCEDURE

Furniture finishing is not difficult when the wood surface has been properly prepared in advance. Unsatisfactory results will be encountered only when: first, there is inadequate sanding; second, each progressive coat is worked before it is thoroughly dry. Contrary to popular belief, there are no "tricks of the trade." Each kind of material used will react the same way for the hobbyist as for the professional. There is only one advantage in favor of the professional—because of his familiarity with the materials to be used and his experience in handling them, he has much more confidence in what will be the end result. Let me say again what is of prime importance —should there be any doubt about the wood surface being ready for finish, sand again until all doubts are removed.

Oil stain. We will recommend a stain or combination of stains for each piece illustrated. This suggested color is what we find to be the most popular. We name Sherwin Williams because that is the brand we use exclusively. That statement in no way degrades other brands. Water and spirit stains are not recommended because of the difficulty in application and their tendency to raise the grain.

When the desired stain color has been mixed, brush it on the piece to be finished as you would use paint. How large an area to be stained before wiping depends on relative humidity at the time. Low humidity speeds up the drying process—high humidity retards it. Also, another point to consider is how many inside corners, moldings, etc. will slow the wiping process. An average piece of furniture will require about the same length of time for wiping as for staining. The stained area should be wiped with a clean cloth as soon as the first brushed portion loses its wet look. Wipe with the grain wherever possible. Use care when wiping the final strokes so that no cloth-weave patterns of excess stain remain on the wood. If the piece of furniture is large, requiring repeated stained-and-wiped areas, the newly stained area may join or even lap the previously stained area without detriment. Caution should be used when standing the piece aside for drying. Hand prints on a newly stained surface will be quite noticeable. Follow-up operations in the finishing process will be carried out with much greater ease and satisfactory results if each coat of material is allowed to dry overnight. Do not hurry this process—it pays.

Wash coat of shellac. After the stain has dried overnight, cut a good grade of white shellac (Bull's Eye brand preferred) half-and-half with alcohol. We will assume here that no spray equipment or knowledge of its use is available. Provide a good-quality long-bristle brush to apply the cut shellac. Unlike paint which may be "brushed in," this wash coat of shellac must be applied with as few brush strokes as are necessary to coat the entire surface evenly.

Quarter a sheet of 7/0 garnet finishing paper (discussed under *Sandpaper*), three-fold rather than fold in half a one-quarter sheet. This method provides more traction on the surfaces (paper to paper) to prevent slippage and consequent crushing.

There need be no doubt as to when the shellac is dry. If the dust created when sanding the shellac coat adheres to the paper as spots of gum, the surface is not ready for sanding. Wait until a dry white powder which does not stick to the paper is produced. Sand just enough to remove all raised wood fibers, leaving a smooth surface, pleasing to the touch.

Dull lacquer. For those familiar with spray equipment, two or more coats may now be applied. Sand between coats with 7/0 paper that has been used to a point where it is crushed and therefore soft. Lacquer is recommended only for spraying.

We will discuss materials suitable for brush use in much more detail.

Shellac may be used as a final build-up material. It is tough and durable but has these negative points: It will watermark if not wiped dry reasonably soon. It is more difficult to brush on evenly than materials with slower-drying properties.

Spar varnish of the quick-drying variety dries slowly enough to brush on evenly. When using fast-dry materials the objective is not to shorten elapsed time but to lessen the opportunity for airborne dust to settle and imbed itself into the soft finish. Varnish is one of two ideal build-up materials when applied with a brush. The other is a choice of a number of brand names featuring plastic coatings.

Plastic coatings. This group of material, compared to traditional varnish, is a new development. Each brand has the plastic characteristics of body, toughness, mark resistance, and is smooth-flowing when applied by brush.

The number of coats applied over the sanded shellac wash coat is a matter of choice. We recommend at least two to prevent moisture from getting underneath and causing a rough surface in spots.

Regardless of which material is used for build-up, each coat except the final one must be sanded with well worn 7/0 paper.

Let the final coat dry until there is no doubt of its hardness. Your patience will be rewarded with a much better rub-down job.

Rub with the grain, holding a pad of 3/0 steel wool. Position the surface to be rubbed between you and a window or lamp; by so doing, the light reflection will show clearly when a smooth satin sheen is achieved. Do not rub more than is necessary to get the desired result. Follow up with a furniture wax or polish. All these preparations should be thoroughly wiped dry after application.

° ② °

Dovetailing

Dovetailing, wherever it can possibly be used, will add distinction to your handiwork and is the best method for corner joinery. It may come as a surprise to find how little extra effort is necessary to make this interesting joint compared to an ordinary milled joint.

Dovetailing is restricted to corner work where the grain of the wood runs to the corner in both pieces to be joined. The most common examples are: drawers where fronts and backs can be joined to the sides; desk-case top to sides; blanket-chest front and back to sides. There are many other instances where dovetailing can be employed. It cannot be used where the wood grain runs parallel with the corner to be joined, such as a front corner of the cove cupboard illustrated on page 45.

To make the following instructions more understandable, a page of illustrations is added here for study. We chose a drawer for illustration because the parts are probably more readily identifiable.

A drawer should be worked on only after the intended compartment is prepared to receive it. Start drawer construction by first finish-sizing the front to fit the intended opening. Cut the back piece the same length as the front, but in width, cut only from the intended position of the groove milled to receive the bottom panel to the drawer front top edge. The purpose of this is to leave open (from the back) the grooves to receive the bottom panel at the proper time.

Saw to finish-size two side pieces, length 3/4″ less than depth of drawer opening, width same as height of drawer front.

The drawer illustrated is a small one (2″ high) so the front thickness is only 1/2″. Sides and back are of 5/16″ thick wood.

Next, mill a groove 1/4″ wide by 5/32″ deep the full length of each side piece and the back surface of the front. This groove is to be measured from the bottom edge 1/8″ to starting edge of groove; this will place the top edge of groove 3/8″ up from drawer bottom edge. Illustration shows this work completed.

Prepare for dovetailing by setting a scratch gauge to the thickness of drawer side wood, 5/16″. Scratch lines on the front piece as indicated on

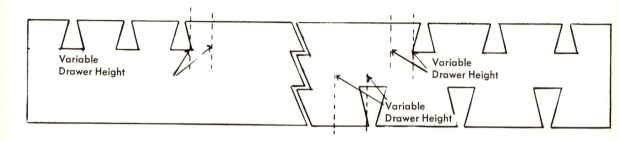

Variable Drawer Height

Variable Drawer Height

Variable Drawer Height

left illustration, i.e. on drawer front ends from back to front, and on back surface from ends toward the center.

Keep the same gauge setting and scratch-mark both flat surfaces at each end of the side and back pieces. You will understand the need for marking both surfaces as work progresses.

Making templates for dovetailing is so quickly done that a new template for each size drawer is not unreasonable. Contrary to your first impression, accurate measurement is unimportant because variation between tails or varying widths of tails will be duplicated exactly when marking the male (front and back) and female (sides) with the same template.

We make templates of any thin sheet metal available, steel, brass, or aluminum. Select a piece of sheet metal large enough to lay out four different-size dovetail patterns, one on each corner. Set a bevel gauge to the approximate angle of cutouts on template illustrated, an angle that will produce a wedge shape about 3/32″ at the template edge and 1/4″ at a line 5/16″ deep. The depth of tail layout should be the thickness of drawer side wood. As the height of drawers increases, so should the distance between tails, within a certain bracket. Normal template layout calls for three tails up to 3″ plus; 4″ to 5″, four tails, and so on.

Using a needle-point scriber, scribe a parallel line (in this case) 5/16″ in from the template metal edge. For the 2″ high drawer we are describing, scratch a needle-point mark on the sheet metal about 1/2″ from corner up the long edge. From this mark, measure about 5/8″ and make another mark; again 5/8″ and a third mark. These marks are the centers of three dovetail cutouts. Place the preset bevel gauge on metal edge and scribe a line for one side of a tail cutout. Reverse the gauge and mark for the other side. Repeat to mark remaining two tails.

MULTI-SIZE TEMPLATE

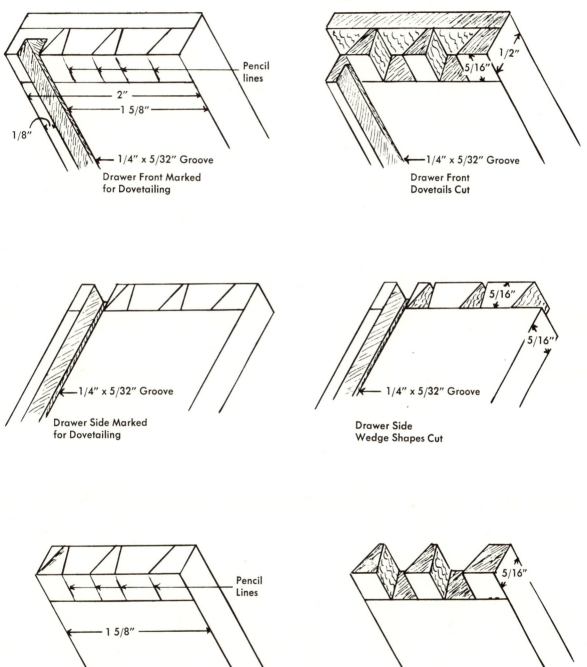

Pencil lines

2"

1 5/8"

1/8"

1/4" x 5/32" Groove

Drawer Front Marked
for Dovetailing

1/2"

5/16"

1/4" x 5/32" Groove

Drawer Front
Dovetails Cut

1/4" x 5/32" Groove

Drawer Side Marked
for Dovetailing

5/16"

5/16"

1/4" x 5/32" Groove

Drawer Side
Wedge Shapes Cut

Pencil Lines

1 5/8"

Drawer Back Marked
for Dovetailing

5/16"

Drawer Back
Dovetails Cut

Cut with tin shears on each line forming the wedge to the 5/16″ parallel line. Lay the sheet metal firmly on a metal block and, using a narrow metal-cutting chisel, chop on the 5/16″ line to remove waste wedge-shaped metal. After removing burrs with a thin file, this particular template is ready for use.

To mark for dovetailing, hold the drawer front in the vise with one end up and the inside surface toward you. Place the template edge exactly on the 5/16″ scribed line. Position the template so that the wide point of the bottom wedge cutout meets the top edge of groove for bottom panel (study drawer front marked for dovetailing illustration). When properly placed, hold template *firmly* in position with left hand and scribe the two side lines of each tail, except the top tail which has only the lower side line scribed. Repeat on the other end of drawer front. The template must be turned over for this marking.

If there should be only one good surface to the back piece, hold this part in the vise with the good surface toward you. Pencil-mark the intended bottom edge of back piece so that when the other end is held for marking, there will be no mistaking on which edge to position the template. Since the back piece is 5/16″ thick, no 5/16″ line must be scribed on the end.

Study the illustration titled "Drawer back marked for dovetailing." Observe that the bottom edge of back piece corresponds to the top edge of groove milled in the front piece. Therefore, position the template edge exactly on the back or far edge of back piece placing the first (or bottom) tail cutout at the lower edge of back piece instead of (as was done when marking the front piece) at the top of groove. Hold firmly so template will not move and mark as instructed for ends of front piece. Repeat on other end, keeping in mind which is the bottom or starting edge—also keep the good surface toward you.

When marking the drawer sides, keep in mind that both ends of each piece are identical and they all match the starting position (top of groove) of template placed on drawer front ends.

Lay a side piece flat on the bench, grooved surface up, place the template edge exactly on and parallel with the side-piece end (see illustration "Drawer side marked for dovetailing"). Position the lower wide point of first cutout directly over the top edge of groove, hold firmly, and mark with scriber both sides of each cutout, except lower side only of the top wedge shape. Repeat on all side ends.

Dovetail marking is now complete except for rough pencil guidelines indicating where to chop (on drawer front) and where to saw (on back piece). At right angle from the wide points of each tail, draw a free-hand pencil line to the scribed 5/16″ line previously scratched on the inside surfaces of both front and back. These lines are necessary because the scribed end lines will not be visible when each piece is conveniently positioned for the work to be done.

Before actual dovetail shaping is started, be sure that this one important condition is met—provide a sturdy, smooth bench top open underneath so a "C" or hand-screw clamp may be used to hold down firmly the drawer front placed with the inside surface up. When clamping the front piece, point the end to be worked on away from your working position. To chop out the waste wood between tails, use a sharp chisel of less width than the distance between two tails which is from one pencil line to the next. Even on larger drawers where the tails are spaced farther apart, a chisel wider than 1/2″ is not recommended for this operation.

Hold the chisel in a perpendicular position parallel to the wood end and not more than 1/8″ in from the wood end. A bite of this small size will easily break away the 1/8″ of wood to the end at each mallet blow. The depth of breakage will show how deep the chisel has cut. Do not cut deeper than the 5/16″ line scribed on the end. Shift the chisel sideways (on the same cutting line) to remove full width waste wood between pencil marks, chop out this section. Repeat 1/8″ bites until the 5/16″ scribed line on back surface is reached. Repeat this same operation between remaining tails and the section from lower tail to the bottom edge. All drawers in the group may be worked to this point of construction progress before proceeding further.

If your supply of chisels should all be of the thick backbone variety, choose a 3/8″ width and grind the heel (back) to a thickness of 1/8″ or less up the shank about one inch. Bevel the sides toward the heel for good clearance.

Vise-grip the drawer front end up, back toward you. Each tail now appears to be a rectangular block instead of a wedge. The objective now is to cut straight down accurately on the waste side of scribed lines. Where considerable wood must be cut away to form one side of the wedge, make small bites that can be done without the use of a mallet. After the vertical walls are cut, hold the chisel horizontally to make a clean-cut right-angle seat to receive the drawer side. The drawer front end should now look like the right illustration marked "Drawer front dovetails cut."

Cutting tails on the back piece is much simpler than on the drawer front since each tail is the full thickness of the back-piece wood. Instead of using a chisel and mallet to cut away the waste wood, a jigsaw may now be used.

To remove waste wood between tails, saw along the pencil lines placed on the back piece for this purpose. Saw to the scribed line, back the saw far enough to swing a tight radius, and cut on the waste side of the scribed line. Swing the back piece to the other side of the saw to remove the waste corner piece left by the radius cut. Repeat between remaining tails.

Viewing the back piece from the end, the tails now look like rectangular blocks instead of wedge shapes. To finish shaping, repeat the series of cuts performed on the drawer front. Compare your finished work with the drawing on right, marked "Drawer back dovetails cut."

Preparing drawer sides to receive dovetails is much more quickly done than front and back pieces. If a jigsaw is available, saw on the waste side of each long line from side-piece end to the 5/16″ scribed line. All that remains to be cut is the wedge angle along the scribed line. To complete the wedge opening, place a side piece (grooved side up) on the solid bench top. Use a sharp chisel of less width than the piece to be cut out. Hold the chisel edge on the 5/16″ line in a perpendicular position and tap with a mallet, cutting about halfway through the wood thickness. Turn over the side piece and finish cutting through from the outside of the drawer side. Compare with illustration marked "Drawer side wedge shapes cut."

·3·

Spice Box

LIST OF MATERIALS

back		20 3/4″ × 7″ × 1/2″
sides	(2)	16″ × 3 1/2″ × 1/2″
top and bottom		7″ × 3 1/2″ × 1/2″
vertical division		15 1/4″ × 3 1/2″ × 5/16″
horizontal divisions	(10)	3″ long 3 1/2″ wide 5/16″ thick
drawer fronts	(12)	2 13/16″ long 2 1/4″ wide 1/2″ thick
drawer sides	(24)	3 1/4″ long 2 1/4″ wide 1/4″ thick
drawer backs	(12)	2 13/16″ long 2″ wide 1/4″ thick
drawer bottoms	(12)	3 1/8″ long 2 9/16″ wide 1/8″ thick
brass drawer knobs	(12)	1/2″ diameter

Much interest is shown in spice boxes. Sizes and shapes are of an infinite variety. Kind of wood used may be walnut, cherry or knotty pine. It is possible that a combination of woods will serve well a particular decorative idea.

We illustrate here a popular-size box made of knotty pine. Without too much mental effort, overall size, shape, or number of drawers can be changed because all construction details remain the same—only dimensions need to be refigured.

If the box is to be made of knotty pine, 1/2″ thick wood can be procured easily from your lumber dealer.

Cut the side pieces to finish size. Prepare also the vertical-division piece exactly the same length and width of the sides. This extra length simplifies milling the horizontal-division slots.

Before milling slots, cut to finish size the top and bottom. Also, enough wood 3 1/2″ wide for ten horizontal-division pieces. The top and bottom are finish thickness. It is now necessary to saw to 5/16″ thickness the vertical-division piece and the length (or lengths) provided for horizontal divisions.

Lay off in pencil the surface of a side piece chosen for the inside. First, mark 1/2″ from each end—then divide the remaining distance into

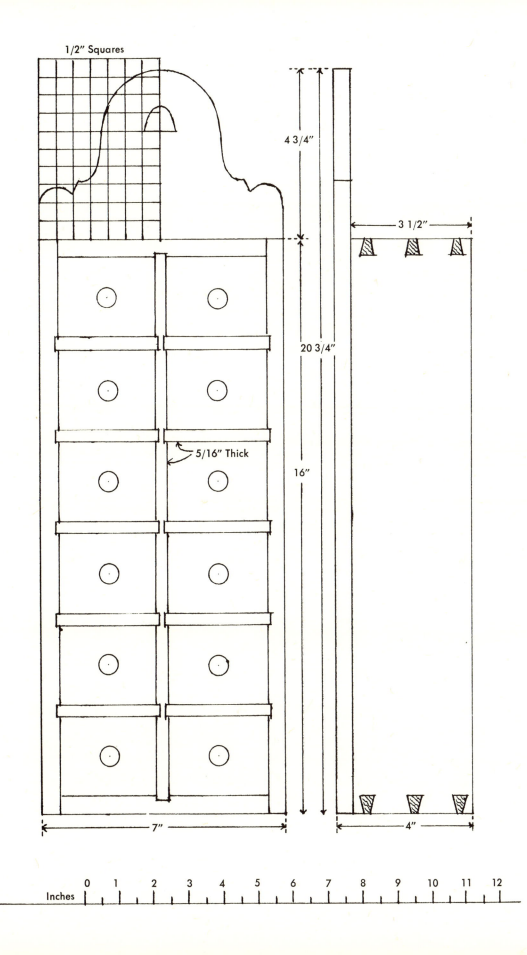

1/2" Squares

4 3/4"

3 1/2"

20 3/4"

5/16" Thick

16"

7"

4"

0 1 2 3 4 5 6 7 8 9 10 11 12

Inches

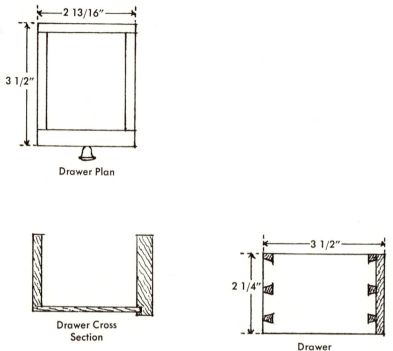

Drawer Plan

Drawer Cross
Section

Drawer
Side View

six equally spaced parts (providing for five 5/16″ dividers). These spaces should measure approximately 2 1/4″.

If you have a multiple cutter dado head for your saw table, put together a 5/16″ width. Set the head for 3/32″ depth. Adjust the ripping fence to cut exactly on each layout line from each end on the inside surface of the side pieces only. Do not forget to dado *both* sides of the vertical piece on each measurement setup. Should it be necessary to use a saw for this operation, many more measurement setups will be required. Finally, dado the same-size slots exactly in the center of the top and bottom pieces (inside surface only).

Dovetail the case corners next. Follow the instructions in dovetailing procedure as applied to back of drawer corners. A template for this width and wood thickness can be made easily, if none on hand is suitable.

When dovetailing is completed, coat the "tails" with glue and assemble the case. Determine exactly how much wood must be cut off *each* end of the center vertical division to make it fit snugly into place. Cut to fit—glue in place. Check the case with a square—if necessary, use hand pressure one way or the other to bring it into line. Carefully set aside for glue hardening.

Measure exactly and cut the horizontal-division pieces for a neat fit. Coat the slots of each division with glue and insert the divider before gluing the next section.

Prepare the back next. The illustration calls for a piece 20 3/4″ × 7″ × 1/2″. The bottom end of this piece must be squared. Lay off the top end as illustrated in 1/2″ squares; draw in the outline; saw to the line. Bore a 1/2″ hanger hole—flair out and flatten the bottom as shown (use a jigsaw for this purpose). Finish-sand sawed edges. Finish-sand the top part of front surface that will show when box is completed.

Clearance-bore four holes for 1″ #5 flathead wood screws 1/4″ in from the edge of the back piece (shown on illustration)—a clearance hole about 2″ in from each side edge of back piece measured so screws will enter the center of wood thickness of top and bottom pieces. Before attaching case to back, finish-sand the case top only. Attach with screws. Finish-sand case sides and bottom.

Prepare strips of wood the indicated widths and thicknesses shown on material list for twelve drawers. Saw 1/8″ × 1/8″ grooves 1/8″ up from the bottom edge of both the side and front pieces to provide slots for insertion of drawer bottoms. Square to length twelve drawer fronts and backs slightly less than the width of drawer openings, twenty-four drawer sides 1/4″ less than the depth of drawer openings. Follow through the complete instructions for drawer dovetailing. Assemble. Finally cut to size 1/8″ thick drawer bottoms, insert, and hold in place with thin brads through bottom wood into the drawer back.

Sand each drawer—sides, front, top and bottom edges—to fit freely into its own compartment. Mark each drawer back and its own compartment consecutively so each may be replaced without guess work.

Fit with 1/2″ brass knobs after wood finishing.

THE STAIN COMBINATION RECOMMENDED IS

> 3/4 English oak
> 1/8 Danish walnut
> 1/8 American cherry

·4·

Fireside Match Box

List of Materials

Rough Measurements

back board		21 1/4″ × 6″ × 1/2″
sides	(2)	15 1/2″ × 3 1/4″ × 1/2″
front		11″ × 6″ × 1/2″
bottoms	(2)	5 1/2″ × 3 1/4″ × 1/2″
drawer front		6″ × 3 1/4″ × 3/4″

1/4″ thick wood for drawer sides and back
1/8″ wood for drawer bottom
1/2″ black iron knob

We call this a fireside match box although originally boxes of this general type were used, more often than not, to hold long stem clay pipes. The drawer at bottom held loose tobacco. This piece will look good if made of pine, walnut, or cherry, although it seems to be particularly suited to pine.

Start with the back board. Rip to 5 1/2″ width—square the bottom end. Measure and mark the taper. Start at the bottom corners (5 1/2″ width), measure up 14 1/2″—square a line across at this point. Mark a center line from top to bottom. At the 14 1/2″ cross line, mark 1 3/4″ and 2 1/4″ out on each side of the center line. Use a straight edge to mark lines from bottom corners to the 4 1/2″ width at the 14 1/2″ line. From the 14 1/2″ line to the top (20 1/4″) lay off the back board into 1/2″ squares on one side of the center line. Follow the shape as outlined on drawing. Band-saw this entire side. Flip over the waste wood for marking the other side—band-saw.

Bore a 1/2″ hanger hole, placed as indicated on drawing. Shape the lower sides and bottom of hole on the jigsaw.

Finish-size two side pieces to 14 1/2″ × 2 3/4″ × 1/2″. Lay off 1/2″ squares from top 3 1/2″ down on one of the pieces. Copy the outline from the drawing onto the squared area. Brad the two sides together placing the nails in the waste wood area—band-saw or jigsaw.

Make a 1/2″ dado setup on the bench-saw arbor, raise the cutters to a depth of 3/32″. Down on the drawing are two bottoms, one above the drawer opening and the other below. Run the lower grooves flush with the squared bottom edges of the side pieces (be sure to choose the surfaces that will result in a pair—one right and one left). Reset the fence to cut the upper grooves 3″ from the bottom edges—check with drawing.

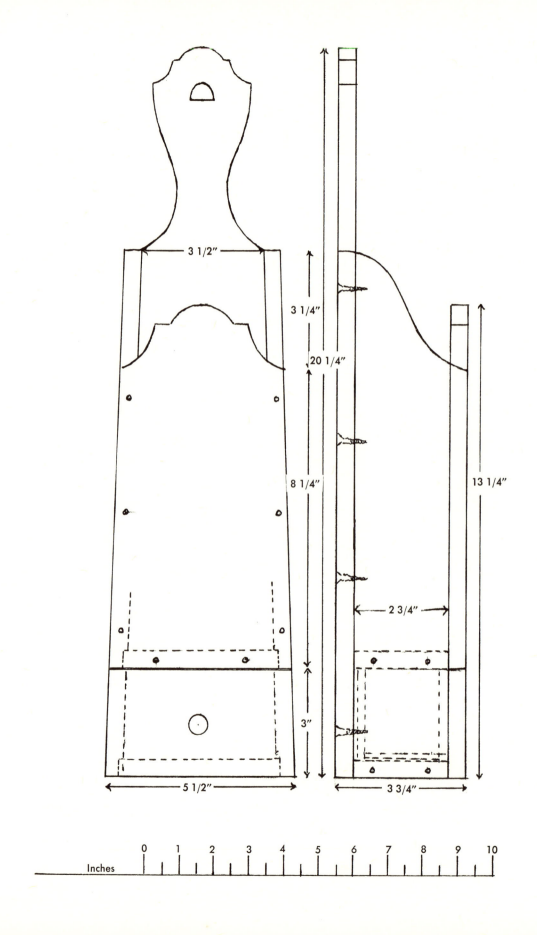

3 1/2"

3 1/4"

20 1/4"

8 1/4"

13 1/4"

2 3/4"

3"

5 1/2"

3 3/4"

Inches 0 1 2 3 4 5 6 7 8 9 10

Before cutting the bottom pieces, accurate measuring will be simplified if the sides are permanently attached to the back. As indicated on drawing, bore four 5/32″ holes along each side of the back 1/4″ in from the edge. Finish-sand the front surface of the back panel. Finish-sand the inside surfaces of the side pieces. Grip one side piece in the vise, back edge up— carefully glue this edge. Place the back piece in position (bottom edge flush with bottom edge of side piece), side edge flush with outside surface of side piece. Seat four 7/8″ #4 wood screws. Repeat with the other side.

Now carefully measure for the two bottoms. There will be a slight variation. The lower one is wider. Rip a piece of 1/2″ pine 2 3/4″ wide,

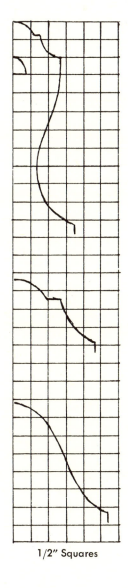

1/2″ Squares

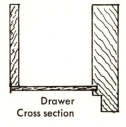

Drawer
Side View

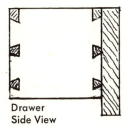

Drawer
Cross section

square the ends of a piece for the upper bottom. The taper angle is so slight that a 90° edge cut is still permissible. If the sliding fit is tight, sand a little at the ends—glue the grooves, slide bottom in and seat against the back. Fit the lower bottom in like manner, although, in this case there are not two walls to hold the piece in place, so when it is positioned, bore two 3/16″ holes through each side and into the bottom wood to a depth of 1 1/4″. If these holes are bored on an angle, the holding properties of the dowels will be greatly increased. Coat the holes with glue, drive in extra long dowels—the excess may be cut off after glue sets. The side view on drawing should clear up any possible confusion.

The front panel should be cut to finish-length but oversize in width, 10 1/4″ long by about 5 3/4″ wide. Lay it in place with the bottom end covering the upper bottom piece. Pencil-mark the overhang along side panels. Band-saw. Mark a center line from top to bottom. On one side mark 1/2″ squares from top down 2″. Copy out-line on drawing. Band-saw. Flip over the waste piece to mark second side. Band-saw. Finish-sand the inside surface of front panel.

Run a thin line of glue on the front edges of side and upper bottom pieces. Accurately position front panel—use two "C" clamps to keep it from shifting; bore 3/16″ holes for dowels as indicated on drawing—glue holes and drive in dowels. Because of the angled band-saw endings of sides and front, where the two join, hand tools must be used to blend the angles into a pleasing ending.

The drawer front can be sized by ripping a 3/4″ piece to fit from the lower edge of the front panel to the bottom of the box. Lay it in place and mark along each side. After band-sawing each side line, the front should follow the box outline but will be raised above the front surface 1/4″. Rabbet out the back surface on sides and bottom a strong 1/2″ in width and 1/4″ from back to front. Trial-fit into opening—there should be about 1/16″ play up and down and sideways.

Cut two side members of 1/4″ wood in height to match the back of the drawer front and in length to leave about 1/8″ clearance at the case back. The drawer back will be sized to match the back of front piece, except 1/4″ less in height. Cut 1/8″ × 1/8″ grooves into sides and front 1/4″ up from bottom edge of sides and 1/4″ plus 1/2″ from bottom of drawer front. Dovetail, following chapter on dovetailing. After assembly, slide 1/8″ bottom in place and brad into back. Finish-sand all band-sawed edges, slide drawer in place and sand all surfaces, including back and bottom.

THE STAIN MIXTURE FOR PINE IS

3/4 English oak
1/8 Danish walnut
1/8 American cherry

·5·

Spoon Rack

LIST OF MATERIALS

1/2″ thick wood throughout

back	12 1/2″ wide × 17 3/4″ long
two sides	2 3/4″ wide × 12 3/4″ long
top shelf	1 7/8″ wide × 12 1/2″ long
rack shelf	1 7/8″ wide × 11 3/4″ long
lift lid	3 5/8″ wide × 12 1/2″ long
bottom	2 3/4″ wide × 12 1/2″ long
box front	2 3/4″ wide × 12 1/2″ long

Spoon racks are always popular with home woodworkers. They may be made of other kinds of wood but knotty pine rates number one.

Size varies a great deal according to the number of spoons to be displayed. A rack may be made wider with the same height; or higher, providing for two rack shelves instead of one, retaining the six-spoon width. The rack design illustrated has a knife box constructed as a base.

Every lumber dealer stocks #2 common white pine (knotty pine) ready-dressed four sides and of 3/4″ thickness. He will probably allow you to choose a board with numerous small, solid knots. This knot pattern is ideal for furniture work. After making your selection, have him plane the board to 1/2″. We suggest eight inches as being the best average width for knotty pine boards (dressed width 7 5/8″). The dealer will no doubt stock up to 12″ widths but if these wider boards are used, they must be worked quickly or great care should be taken to turn over the board frequently to prevent warping.

Your shop equipment should include a number of bar clamps for gluing two or more boards together for greater width. The first action to take in this case is: saw two lengths of an 8″ board 18 3/4″ rough length. Glue these together, being sure their planed edges are square and straight.

Rather than work the resultant back board to finish size at this time, prepare the side pieces to finished length and over-all width. Saw or dado a 1/2″ wide by 1/8″ deep groove 4 1/4″ from the top end of each piece to receive the rack shelf. Lay one piece on top of the other, matching groove to groove. Positioning the parts in this way will result in a right and a left side after shaping the front edge, as illustrated. To keep the two sides aligned, seat two 3/4″ brads in what will be waste wood.

Lay off the top surface in 1/2″ squares and, using the drawing as a

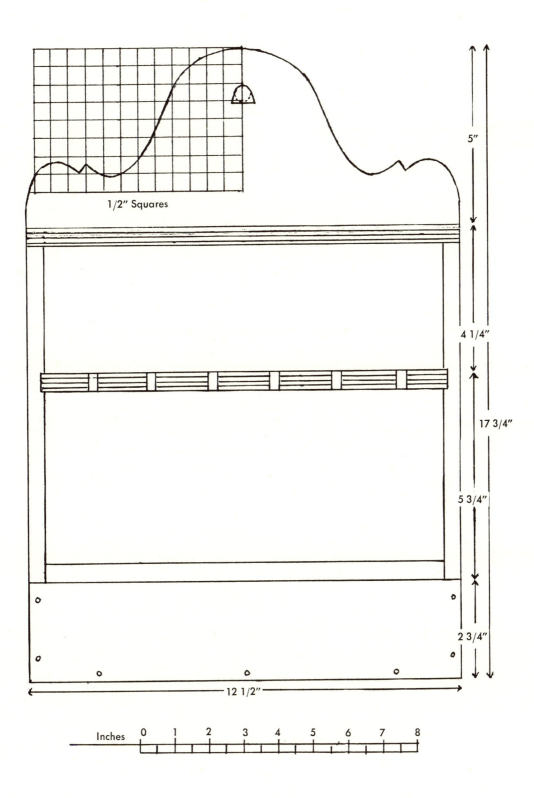

1/2" Squares

5"

4 1/4"

17 3/4"

5 3/4"

2 3/4"

12 1/2"

Inches   0   1   2   3   4   5   6   7   8

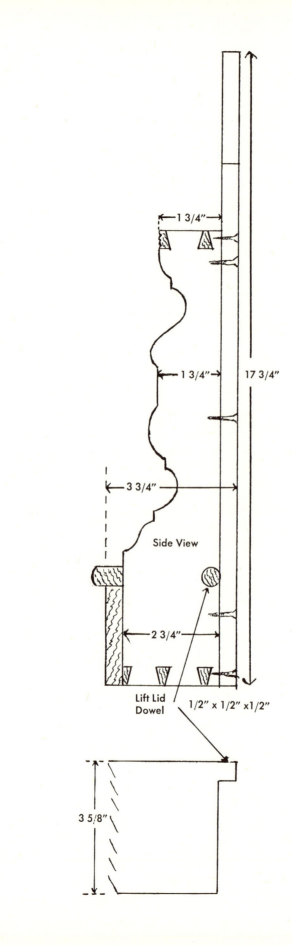

1 3/4"

17 3/4"

1 3/4"

3 3/4"

Side View

2 3/4"

Lift Lid
Dowel

1/2" x 1/2" x 1/2"

3 5/8"

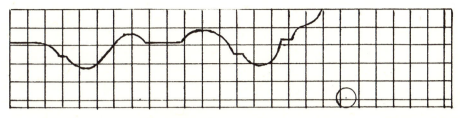

1/2" Squares

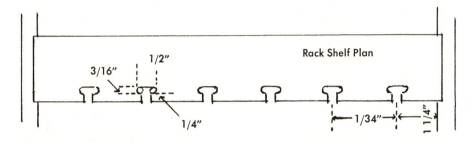

3/16"
1/2"
1/4"
Rack Shelf Plan
1/34"
1 1/4"

guide, pencil in the curves as illustrated. Also position, mark, and bore a 1/2" hole for lift-lid dowels. Band-saw or jigsaw to the penciled line. Smooth the sawed edges and inside surface with coarse, then fine, sandpaper.

Next, finish-size three cross members. Top 12 1/2" × 1 3/4". Rack shelf 11 3/4" × 1 3/4". Bottom 12 1/2" × 2 3/4". Study well the treatise on dovetailing. Become familiar with progressive steps as applied to the case in hand, which is comparable to the joining of a drawer side to drawer back. The drawer back is represented by top and bottom members, the drawer sides by the present spoon-rack sides.

After completion of the dovetail joints, set a common scratch gauge to 1/8". Scratch deep lines on the front edge of top and rack shelves. Reset gauge to 1/4" (the center of wood thickness) and scratch a center line on each piece. These scratched grooves are the bases for four decorative beads on the front edge of each piece.

Make a sanding block in the following manner: start with a piece of wood about 4" long × 2" wide × 1/4" thick. Plane one of the 4" sides to a long taper ending in a feather edge. Smooth and deepen each scratched line by gripping one thickness of 3/0 sandpaper over the feather edge of the sand block—align in a rough groove—use a back-and-forward motion to complete work on each groove.

Lay off, on the top surface of the rack shelf, spoon slots as indicated on shelf plan. The slots will be neater and more uniform if you drill a 3/16″ hole through the wood thickness at each end of what will be the 1/2″ long slot. Follow with fine blade jigsaw to complete slot shape according to plan. Finish-sand both sides.

Size, shape, and finish-sand the lift lid. Start with a piece 12 1/2″ × 3 5/8″ × 1/2″ thick. Mark and remove from each end, by sawing, 1/2″ long pieces of waste wood leaving intact bosses 1/2″ × 1/2″ × 1/2″ (spoon rack drawing). On the end of each boss, roughly pencil in a circle. Chisel to the line to form a 1/2″ diameter dowel. Work these dowels down in size until they fit freely into the holes bored through side pieces to receive them. The long back edge must, of necessity, be planed to match one half of the dowels at each end. The front edge of the lid should be crowned as indicated on the drawing. This may be done with a plane. Sand coarse and fine.

Coat the (dove) tails with glue, top and bottom pieces; lay one side piece on a work table (inside surface up); position the top shelf and press into tail openings; repeat with the bottom piece. Insert a lift-lid dowel into the hole provided. Position the other side piece (inside surface down) on the cross members; seat the dovetails. Do not, at this time, insert rack shelf into receiving slots. Check the assembled frame for true 90° corners. If necessary, adjust before glue sets. Carefully set aside for glue-hardening time.

Now match back-board width to the actual width of the assembled frame. Saw the bottom end to a squared line. Mark with a squared line the top end 17 3/4″ finished length. Draw a vertical center line in pencil on the back board. From the center line to the left edge, draw a line paralleling the top line, 4″ down. Fill in this rectangle with 1/2″ blocks as shown on drawing. Use the drawing as a guide for imposing the curved line forming half of the top edge design. Also mark and bore the 1/2″ hanger hole. Flair out the bottom half of this hole as shown.

Band-saw or jigsaw the curved top line. Lay over the waste piece as you would turn a page. Outline and saw to this new line. Sand to finish smoothness the entire top edge. Sand the front surface of the back board, coarse and fine.

Drill holes for 1″ × #6 flathead wood screws in back board, three down each side—two each to fasten the top shelf and the bottom. Lay the frame work upside-down, position the back board (front surface down) on the frame, sides and bottom edges flush with corresponding frame outline. Hold in position and seat all screws.

Fit (if necessary) the rack shelf. Coat each slot with glue and press the shelf into position, seating it firmly against the back board.

Finish-size the piece that will form the front surface of the knife box.

Sand the top edge only. Position and hold with clamps. Drill 3/16″ holes for dowels as indicated on drawing, each hole through the face board and at least 1/2″ into the frame members. Slant the drill as you would when driving a "tow nail." This method has much better holding effect.

All that remains to complete this piece for finish is to sand the outside surfaces of the sides, front board, bottom, and (optional) the back.

THE STAIN MIXTURE FOR PINE IS

    3/4 English oak
    1/8 Danish walnut
    1/8 American cherry

°6°

Candle Stand

LIST OF MATERIALS

legs	(4)	1 1/8″ × 1 1/8″ × 27 1/2″
skirting	(4)	5/8″ × 2 3/4″ × 9″
top		10 1/2″ × 10 1/2″ × 1/2″
gallery	(4)	3/16″ × 7/8″ × 10″
tray, incl. batten		1/2″ × 6″ × 9 1/4″
slide runners	(2)	3/4″ × 1″ × 8 1/2″
top attach battens	(2)	5/8″ × 3/4″ × 7 3/4″
brass knob		1/2″ dia.

The descriptive name, "candle stand," does not detract in the least from the table's interesting size, proportions, and possible uses. The most ideal spot for this table is a small area that cannot accommodate a larger piece. It can be used for supporting a small reading lamp and ashtray or a purely decorative object.

The table used for illustration is of figured maple. Equally suitable would be cherry, walnut, or mahogany. Pine is not recommended because of the table's delicate proportions.

The first parts to prepare are the legs. Mill them to finish size—1 1/8″ × 1 1/8″ × 27 1/2″. Tapering is done best on the jointer by laying a leg blank on the jointer bed in a position where the cutters will start the taper 3 3/4″ down from the top. How deep the jointer is set to cut will determine the number of passes necessary on each of the leg's four sides to reduce the lower end to 5/8″ × 5/8″. Repeat with the remaining three legs.

Next, four skirt pieces should be prepared, each piece 5/8″ thick, 2 3/4″ wide, and a rough length of 10 inches. Set the cross cut gauge to 2° off 90°. Saw each end of each piece on this angle, measuring for a top (or short) length of 9 inches.

If a multiple cutter dado head is included in your equipment, set up the two side cutters with a 1/4″ spacer between. Raise the assembly to a cutting height of 5/8 inch. Set the ripping fence to cut a 1/4″ shoulder on the front surface (see "Plan—leg and skirt detail"). Pass each end of each piece, front surface against the ripping fence and in an end-up position, over the dado setup. Replace the dado cutters with a combination or a crosscut saw blade, setting the fence to cut shoulder waste wood leaving a tenon on each·end 5/8″ long by 1/4″ thick. This means two depth settings: 1/4″ for the front shoulders, 1/8″ for the back. It is much easier, because of the slight angle, to cut a 1/4″ shoulder top and bottom on each end with a band saw or handsaw.

Choose the two inside right-angle surfaces of each leg; scratch-gauge a center line, 3/8" from what will be the outside corner of each mortised surface (leg and skirt detail). Pencil-mark the mortise ending 1/4" down from the top of the leg and make another mark 2 1/2" down from the top, indicating the lower mortise end. Bore in line a series of 1/4" holes 11/16" deep (see mortise and tenon detail) using the scratch gauge mark for bit center. Repeat with each leg.

To square out the mortises for tenon fitting, use hand pressure on a 1/2" or 3/4" sharp chisel for the long walls. Use a 3/16" wide chisel to square the ends. Try each joint for snug fit before final assembly.

All four skirt pieces being the same length, choose the best one for the front. Mark for the sliding-tray slot as shown on the drawing, 6" wide by 1/2" high. Saw to the line. Finish-sand the entire mortised surfaces of each leg now, because there are no obstructions at this stage.

The legs and skirt pieces may now be assembled into a single unit. Coat the walls of each mortise with glue; coat lightly the long surfaces of each tenon; press each tenon into its mortise by hand. Adjust a bar clamp to span the front and back legs on one side. Insert, at the clamp jaws, thin pieces of wood to prevent the jaws from marking the legs. Tighten clamp. Repeat on the other side. Now adjust two bar clamps to span the side clamps. Position them parallel to front and back; tighten for joint inspection and true 90° corners. Should the unit be out of square, shift one or both clamps slightly off parallel; retighten and check with a square. Allow overnight glue-setting time.

Next, fit two 3/4" × 3/4" by the distance between the front and back legs on each side (see cross section on drawing) for the purpose of top attachment with screws. After milling a 2° angle on one 3/4" face of each piece, bore and countersink a screw hole about 1" from each end of each piece for fastening to skirts (flush with the top edge of skirt). Attach with one-inch #6 or 7 wood screws.

All outside surfaces of legs and skirts may now be sanded, coarse and fine. Any possible uneven joints of skirts and legs should be sanded out with coarse paper. Sand with the grain of skirt pieces and follow up (removing cross scratches) on the leg surfaces sanding with the leg grain. The same procedure should be followed with 3/0 finishing paper.

The top board should be made up of 2 or more pieces 1/2" thick by 11 1/2" long, glued edge to edge, finish sizing to 10 1/2" × 10 1/2". Rough-sand the underneath and top surfaces. Set up the dado for 3/16" grooves (one 1/8" side cutter and 1/16" raker). Set the fence to leave 1/4" of top surface outside of the 3/16" groove (see gallery plan and detail). Adjust for a depth setting of 1/8". Mill each of four grooves no closer than 1/4" to the bordering right angle edges. Cut out to depth with a 1/8" chisel the dado radius endings at each corner. Slightly round the edges of top board (gallery and plan detail) using a hand plane. Rough-and finish-sand the edges. Finish-sand the top surface.

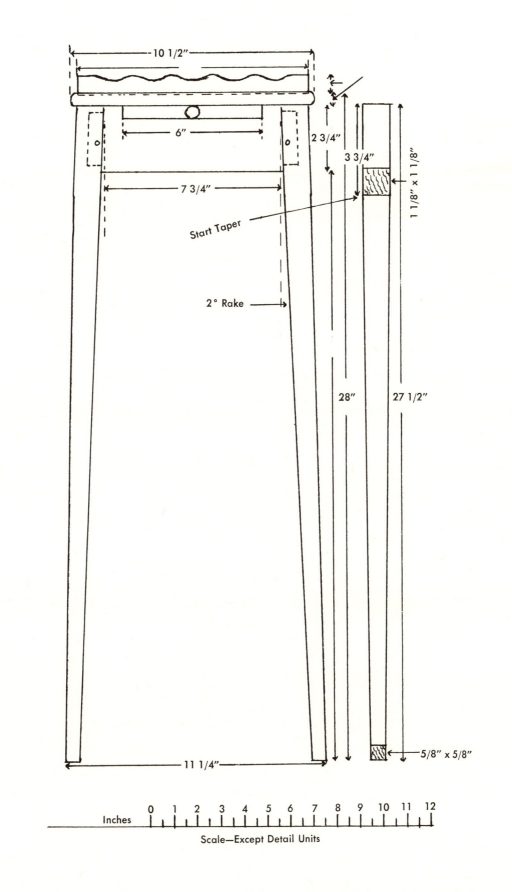

10 1/2"

6"

2 3/4"

3 3/4"

1 1/8" x 1 1/8"

7 3/4"

Start Taper

2° Rake

28"

27 1/2"

11 1/4"

5/8" x 5/8"

Inches 0 1 2 3 4 5 6 7 8 9 10 11 12

Scale—Except Detail Units

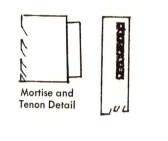

Mortise and
Tenon Detail

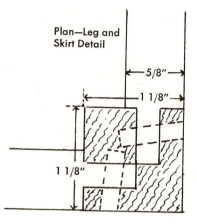

Plan—Leg and
Skirt Detail

5/8"

1 1/8"

1 1/8"

Mill gallery strips (superimposed on 1/2" × 1" blocks, shown on drawing) to a snug fit in the 3/16" grooves; saw strips 7/8" wide; miter ends for an exact fit in each groove. Stack the four pieces, all edges even and brad together (two places) in what will be waste wood. Lay off the top surface into blocks (see drawing). Pencil-line the scallop-top edge. Band-saw or jigsaw to this line. Sand the scalloped top edge of all four pieces. Rough- and finish-sand inside and outside surfaces of the gallery pieces.

Bore vertical screw holes through the 3/4" × 3/4" top attachment pieces, position each hole close to the horizontal-skirt attachment screws.

Center the base assembly on the top board in an upside-down position. Be sure the top wood grain runs from side to side rather than front to back. Attach with 1" # 6 or 7 wood screws.

Next, mill the tray-support runners. These are illustrated on the cross section. May be made of a softer wood if so desired, 1" thick by 1 1/8" wide by the distance between front and back skirts. To form runners, saw out the top inside corners 1/2" from the top down and 3/8" wide. Bore two screw holes in each piece. Attach to top board with 1 1/4" #7 wood screws at right angles to the front skirt and in line with the tray opening.

Mill the tray board to fit the opening in width and thickness (grain running from front to back); leave it extra long. Square one end; mill a tongue on this end (the full width of tray board) 3/16" thick by 1/4" long (Sliding tray detail). Mill the front batten, grain running from side to

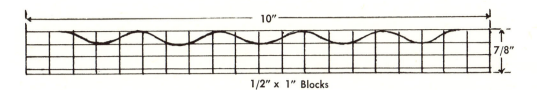

10"

7/8"

1/2" x 1" Blocks

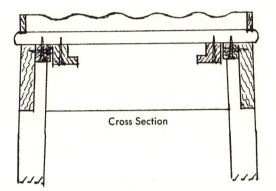

Cross Section

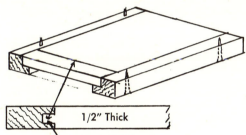

1/2" Thick

1/4" x 3/16" Tongue
Sliding Tray Detail

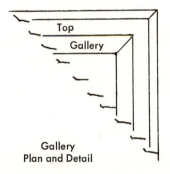

Top

Gallery

Gallery
Plan and Detail

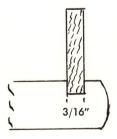

3/16"

side, 2″ wide by 1/2″ thick by about 7″ long. Mill a snug fit groove to receive the tongue. Glue-coat tongue and groove, press together, clamp; allow overnight setting. Mark and saw off the waste batten wood on each side of the tray. Measure exactly the distance from inside back skirt to outside front skirt; square cut the back end of tray to this measurement. Rough-sand all surfaces to get a freely sliding fit. When fitted satisfactorily, finish-sand.

Glue-coat the gallery grooves only; press gallery pieces in place. Sand the sharp gallery corners. Read carefully the suggested finished process.

IF THIS STAND HAS BEEN MADE OF MAPLE, THE PINE STAIN FORMULA CAN BE USED

    3/4 English oak
    1/8 Danish walnut
    1/8 American cherry

·7·

Dry Sink

LIST OF MATERIALS

boards   (7)   1″ × 12″ × 8′
3/8″ wood for drawer sides, back, and bottom
1/4″ plywood 36″ × 36″
H L hinges (black)   2 pairs
knobs   (2)   1″ diameter (black)
magnetic door catch

One must be past middle age to remember dry sinks first hand. The better ones were lined with copper, but most had a sheet-zinc lining. Reproductions made today are without metal linings.

The wood used for this piece is #2 white pine (knotty pine). These boards can be purchased at any lumberyard. They are stocked in all widths and lengths, planed to 3/4″ thickness and edge planed to 3/8″ less than given width, kiln-dried for immediate use.

Start with the base-cabinet side panels—the drawing calls for 17″ wide 29 1/4″ long. Glue up these panels the exact width but 1″ longer to allow for squaring to size. Next, glue boards to make up the shelf and bottom which, incidentally, are the same size— 16 3/4″ wide (exact) × 35 1/2″ long. This measurement is determined by cabinet width of 35 1/2″ less 3/4″ and 3/4″ plus 1/8″ and 1/8″ grooves in side panels for shelf and bottom fitting. Squared finished lengths are 34 1/4″.

The cabinet top, which is also the sink bottom, can be glued to make up a panel 17 3/4″ exact × 47″ long, to be finish-sized to 46″ long.

Rough-sand the five panels on both sides after squaring to respective lengths. The side panels must have 3/4″ wide × 1/8″ deep grooves cut to receive both shelf and bottom; observe blowup on drawing. The bottom grooves are measured, from the bottom up 2″ to 2 3/4″ and the shelf from top down 13″ to 13 3/4″. To form the feet, set a compass to 1 1/4″ radius; center-point the compass for the back feet 3/4″ up from bottom and 3 1/4″ in from back edge; draw a quarter circle. For the front, set the point at 3/4″ up and 2 1/2″ in from front. When the facing stile is attached, the front foot will match the back in width. The top of quarter circle is 2″ up from bottom; draw a straight line from front to back. Bandsaw. Remember these are laid off and cut as a pair, right and left. Rabbet out the inside back edges 1/4″ × 3/8″ for the 1/4″ plywood back panel. Finish-sand the top surfaces of shelf and bottom.

Counterbore 1/2″ diameter by 1/8″ deep for wood screws as indicated on blowup drawing. Bore 11/64″ holes for 1 1/4″ #8 flat head screws. Assemble sides, shelf, and bottom panels.

Mill 2 facing stiles 4″ wide by 29 1/4″ long. These are to be right and left; along the outer edge counterbore for 5 screws—see drawing—bore for #8 screws. Compass in the quadrants to match the side back feet. Bandsaw. Place in position, attach with screws. Along the inner edges and centered over both shelf and bottom, counterbore for #8 screws; bore 11/64″ holes. A 1/2″ plug cutter may be purchased probably in any store that stocks a variety of tools; definitely, a mill supply house will have it. Cut a supply of these plugs; glue the edge of a plug and tap it in over a seated screw. Repeat with all screws ready for covering. Rough-sand the plugs down even with the panel surfaces. Finish-sand front and sides.

The cabinet top 17 3/4″ × 46″ can be placed on the cabinet, an overhang on the left side of 1 3/4″ leaving 8 3/4″ on the right. Mark and counterbore for 3 screws over each side panel to attach the top. Because the cabinet will probably be moved by lifting the top structure, it will be best to use 1 1/2″ #8 screws. One screw into each front stile will also help to strengthen the whole unit. Rough-sand the plugs flush with top surface. Finish-sand.

Wood for superstructure will be given in finished sizes. Always allow one inch in length for squaring to size. The drawing calls for a backboard 8 3/4″ wide by 47 1/2″ long, front piece 4 3/4″ × 47 1/2″ (left side 4 3/4″ × 19 1/4″, right side 11 1/2″ × 19 1/4″). A shoulder must be cut on each end of all pieces for dovetails. The front and back pieces must have an end protruding 3/4″ past the shoulder 1/2″ thick leaving the full length wood on the front surface. The left side piece will be milled the full width; the right side, as the drawing and photo show, is shouldered only 4 3/4″ down from the top. These pieces are milled so as to leave (on the outside surface) 1/2″ × 1/2″ for dovetails. Keep in mind the instructions for the back end of a drawer. Cut the Ogee shape on backboard, marking 1″ squares as indicated on drawing; cut dovetails; coarse- and fine-sand all inside surfaces.

A trial run (without glue) cannot be made with this assembly because the dovetails should be such a close fit that to take the joints apart would break out too much wood. Therefore, go over each piece measuring again to see that the inside size when glued together will match the measurement of the top board, counterbore the wall pieces for 5 screws front and back and 3 screws on ends. Use 1 1/4″ screws through walls and into edges of top board. Glue dovetails and assemble. After overnight setting, slip the wall assembly over the top board, allowing the walls to come down flush with bottom edge of top; fasten with screws, glue, and insert plugs; after glue sets, coarse- and fine-sand all wall surfaces; slightly round, with a draw knife, all wall top edges; finish-sand.

A bottom board will complete the drawer compartment. Measure from cabinet side to inside of right wall; this will be the exact width of board—

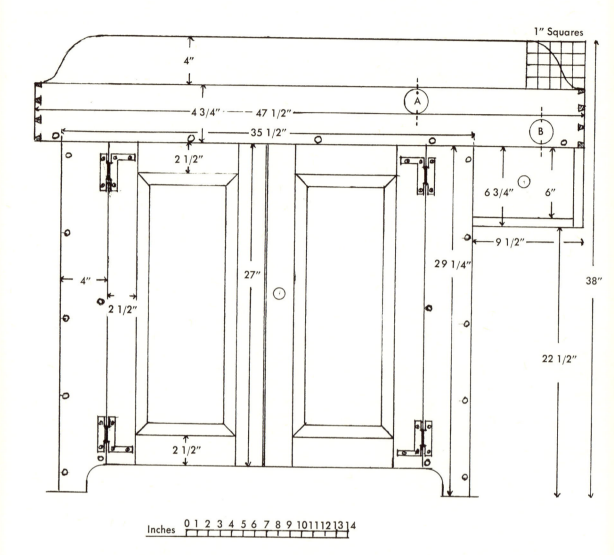

the length is 19 1/4". Counterbore and plug three 1 1/4" screws through the wall; bore and seat 3 screws from the inside of cabinet. A piece of wood either 1/4" or 3/4" thick may be sized to close the back of this compartment; it may be nailed in place after drawer is fitted and stop-blocked.

This drawer has no lip, so to keep it flush on the front, mill the side pieces so that when the drawer is complete it will be 1/2" shorter than the opening; glue on the side walls in back, 1/4" × 1/4" × 2" stop blocks, rubbing them until the glue catches, keeping an unglued side against the drawer-side back edge. This drawer has a 3/4" thick front and 3/8" sides, back and bottom.

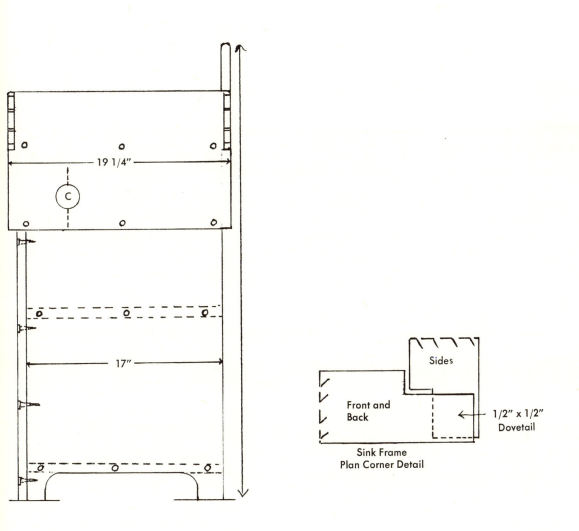

Sides

Front and
Back

1/2" x 1/2"
Dovetail

Sink Frame
Plan Corner Detail

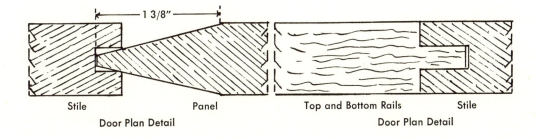

Stile

Panel

Door Plan Detail

Top and Bottom Rails

Stile

Door Plan Detail

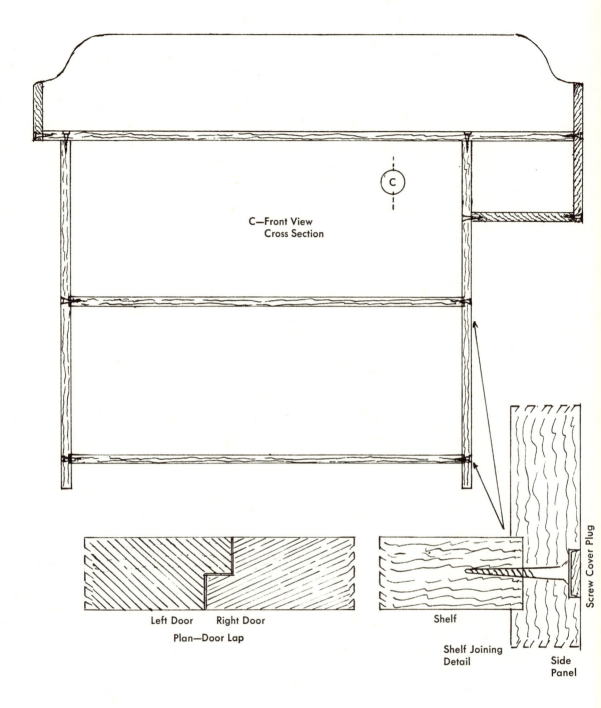

C—Front View
Cross Section

Left Door   Right Door

Plan—Door Lap

Shelf

Shelf Joining
Detail

Side
Panel

Screw Cover Plug

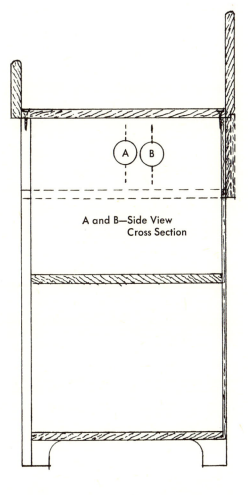

A and B—Side View
Cross Section

When making the doors, first measure the full opening in width and height; take half of the width plus 3/16″ as being the width of each door. The 3/16″ represents one half of a 3/8″ lap in the center when the doors close (drawing blowup).

Mill the door frames next—4 stiles 2 1/2″ wide by measured height which should be 27″. To figure the rails (top and bottom), take the projected door width less 2 1/2″ and 2 1/2″ plus tongues 1/2″ and 1/2″. This is the length of the rails which are also 2 1/2″ wide. Make a pencilled X on one side of all 8 pieces. Use the two outside dado cutters with a 1/4″ spacer between them; raise the cutters to cut a depth of 1/2″; set the fence so that the tongue will be about center of the 3/4″ thick wood. Holding a rail on end (with the X side against the fence), pass it over the dado. Repeat on all rail ends.

Before changing to a saw blade, remove the 1/4" spacer; mount the two end cutters which make up 1/4" for a groove. Using a rail end, set the fence to cut grooves to meet the tongues exactly; raise dado to cut 9/16" in height. Keep X side to the fence and cut about 3" in from each stile end to the full height. Lower dado to cut 5/16" for panel insertion; keep X side to the fence and pass all 8 pieces over the dado (full length). Replace dado with saw blade and set fence to cut 1/2" to the outside of blade. This will leave shoulders on both sides of each tongue 1/2" in from the end.

Assemble one door frame (dry run)—measure for panel plus 1/4" and 1/4" in width and also in height. Glue up panels, if necessary; square to size; tilt the saw blade for bevels on panels (drawing blowup). Coarse- and fine-sand panels, also the grooved edge of each frame part. Coat tongues with glue; assemble each door complete; place in bar clamps; adjust clamps to bring door into square. Overnight drying. Sand front and back frame surfaces. If there is a choice, choose one face for each door; on the right one, rabbet out the back edge (door plan detail) leaving 3/8" × 3/8" for a lap. On the left, leave the lap wood on the back surface. Pass the top edge of each door over the jointer which should be set to cut 1/8"; this is for clearance when doors are mounted flush with the bottom. Finish-sand all edges.

All that remains before staining is to cut to fit the plywood back panel. Hold in place with 1" head nails. Hardware is attached after finishing materials have been applied. The magnetic catch is placed on the right hand door.

SUGGESTED STAIN MIX IS

    3/4 English oak
    1/8 Danish walnut
    1/8 American cherry

Cove Cupboard

LIST OF MATERIALS

boards	(11)	1″ × 12″ × 8′0″
1/4″ plywood 4′ × 8′		
strap hinges	(black)	2 pairs
surface latches	(black)	2

This cupboard, even though easily made, is quite an attractive piece. It got its name from the side cutouts of the open top section. Probably was made originally to fill a space that would not accommodate the larger Dutch cupboard or Welch dresser.

Number 2 white pine (knotty pine) is the best wood to use for this piece. As has been mentioned, knotty pine can be procured easily from any lumber yard and is already dressed to 3/4″ thick and edged to 3/8″ less than the given width. Some board footage may be saved from the suggested quantity in the list of materials by learning just what lengths and widths are available.

All the panels that need to be glued to make up the necessary widths should be prepared before accurate milling is started. The drawing shows side panels 17 1/4″ × 74 1/4″, bottom, shelf, and base top 17″ × 42 3/4″. This measurement is computed by starting with 44″ overall width less 3/4″ and 3/4″ sides plus 1/8″ and 1/8″ for insertion in 3/4″ × 1/8″ grooves. The actual top panel is 16″ × 42 3/4″. The 3 intermediate shelves are 8 3/4″ × 42 3/4″. Gluing up the doors may be deferred until the openings are ready for measurement. Remember to add one inch to the rough length of boards for final squaring to size.

While the side panels are a uniform width, measure for and mill all 3/4″ × 1/8″ grooves. The positions are indicated and measure-marked on drawing. The bottom-board groove is placed to keep the bottom 1/2″ above the floor. Also rabbet out for the 1/4″ plywood back, full length of each side panel (right and left) 1/4″ × 3/8″.

Next, lay off and band-saw the coves. Radii and compass-point marks are indicated on drawing. Counterbore 1/2″ diameter and 1/8″ deep holes for 1 1/2″ #8 screws and plugs. Three screws go through side panels into shelves and bottom where the sides are widest, two screws in the cove area. Mill a plate groove in each cove shelf plus the base top panel. Set up the dado to cut 3/8″ wide × 1/4″ deep, setting the fence 1 1/2″ from the back edge. These grooves may run the full length of shelves but it leaves a better looking job if each groove is started and stopped about 3″ from each end.

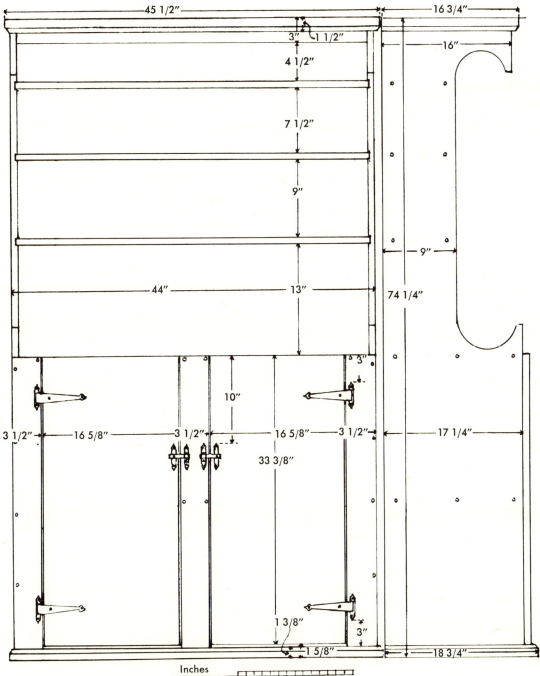

Inches
0 3 6 9

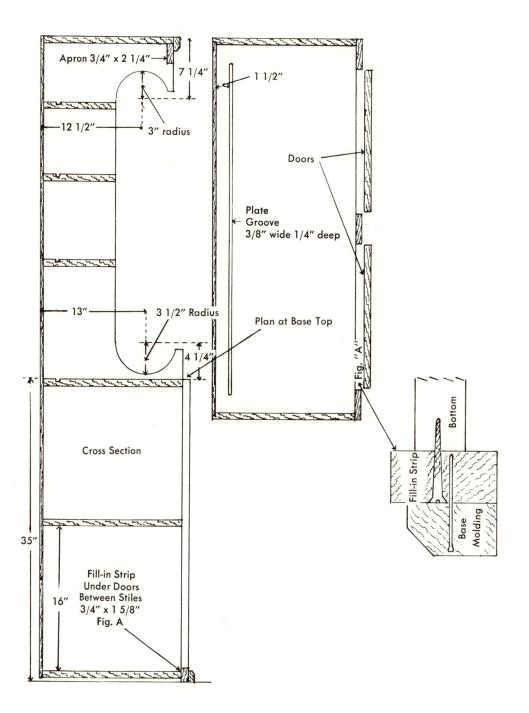

Apron 3/4" x 2 1/4"

7 1/4"

1 1/2"

12 1/2"

3" radius

Doors

Plate
Groove
3/8" wide 1/4" deep

13"

3 1/2" Radius

Plan at Base Top

4 1/4"

Fig. "A"

Cross Section

Bottom

Fill-in Strip

35"

Base Molding

Fill-in Strip
Under Doors
Between Stiles
3/4" x 1 5/8"
Fig. A

16"

All panels are now ready for coarse sanding. The panels to be fine-sanded at this time are: top and bottom surfaces of 3 cove shelves, bottom surface of extreme top, top surface of base top, top surface of lower shelf, top surface of bottom and the inside surfaces of side panels.

The case may now be assembled. Do not rely too much on glue in grooves for strength. The use of glue will only give the case more rigidity which is really worth the effort. Plug all screw holes. Sand front edges of cove shelves, base top and lower shelf, also the cove edge surfaces.

The apron or valance on the top front is fitted between sides and is 2 1/4″ wide × 3/4″ thick (drawing blowup). Counterbore 5 holes for screws through the top panel. Sand the apron on front surface and lower edge. Now 3 stile pieces for the base front 3 1/2″ wide × 35″ long. Those to be used for right and left should have 5 counterbored holes for screws into side panels; also counterbore, near the inside stile edge, one hole over the base top, lower shelf, and the bottom board. When attaching, keep stile edge flush with outside side surface. The one between doors is, of course, centered on the cabinet. Counterbore near the edges and over top, shelf and bottom; fasten with screws and plug. Make fill-in strips—follow the blowup drawing; strips are 1 5/8″ high. Finish-sand stiles and outside side panels.

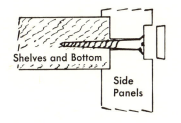

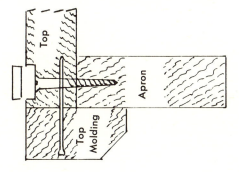

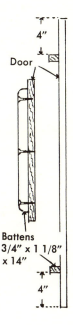

Make enough lineal footage of top and base molding—top measurement is 1 1/2″ × 3/4″, the base 1 3/8″ × 3/4″. As shown on the drawing, set the jointer fence to 45° and a depth of about 1/4″. The top molding will have the lower front edge chamfered; chamfer upper front edge of base molding. Finish-sand moldings before mitering. Attach with finishing nails. Finish-sanding the cupboard top is optional.

Measure accurately both door openings; glue up boards to fit in width plus 1″ extra in length. Next day, square to size less 1/16″ all around; finish-sand all surfaces. Make 2 battens for each door 1 1/8″ × 3/4″ by 2″ less than door width; bore 3 screw holes 11/64″ diameter down through the 1 1/8″ measurement in each batten; countersink, do not counterbore. One inch radius on each top end corner—see drawing which also illustrates battens positions (4″ down from top, 4″ up from bottom). Before attaching, sand all surfaces except bottom which touches the door surface. These battens are necessary to keep the doors from warping. Attach hardware after finishing materials have been applied.

STAIN MIX FOR PINE IS

    3/4 English oak
    1/8 Danish walnut
    1/8 American cherry

·❾·

Late Plank Bottom Chair

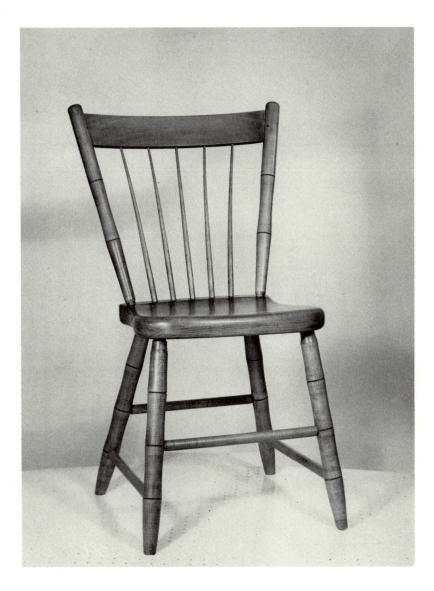

LIST OF MATERIALS

Rough measurements except leg blanks and back posts.

legs	(2)	1 5/8″ × 1 5/8″ × 18 3/4″ long
	(2)	1 5/8″ × 1 5/8″ × 18 1/4″ long
back posts	(2)	1 3/8″ × 1 3/8″ × 21 1/4″ long
seat		1 3/4″ thick × 17″ × 17″
top rail		1 3/4″ thick × 3″ × 19″
spindles	(5)	9/16″ × 9/16″ × 16″ long
stretchers	(4)	7/8″ × 7/8″ × 17″ long

This chair is better than average in design. The refinements built into the back put it a cut above what was common for the original plank bottoms. We are working with three kinds of wood when making a plank bottom— poplar, maple, and hickory or (second choice) white oak for spindles.

First, provide the necessary lumber. Leg stock, back posts, and stretchers are hard maple. Seat and top rail are poplar and, as mentioned, hickory for spindles.

It is most probable that 2″ thick poplar 16″ wide will be unobtainable for the seat. Should you feel uncertain of your ability or lack proper clamps to make this important glue joint, your local planing mill will furnish the lumber and also glue it to the desired width. At the same time, have the mill plane it to 1 3/4″.

Make a seat pattern—especially if a set of chairs is contemplated. Use a stiff, light-colored cardboard (on which inked squares will be visible) to lay out the pattern. Start with a 16″ square. Ink in 1″ square lines over the entire board. Draw in the outline as illustrated on drawing. Mark leg and posthole positions. Also, on the center line place two intersecting points for brace angles—draw straight lines from points to hole centers. Cut pattern board outline. Place pattern on seat plank, being sure to have the wood grain running from right to left; mark outline and (without moving the pattern) use a sharp-pointed awl to press through the pattern board and into the wood as centers for leg and postholes. Plus point intersections for brace angles. Band-saw seat board to outline. Deepen all center points on seat and draw straight brace lines as indicated on drawing and pattern.

The importance of accurately boring leg and postholes cannot be stressed too strongly. Clamp the seat plank firmly on the worktable (distinguished from the bench because it is lower). Should it be necessary to use the bench for this operation, place a wooden box or platform of some kind to stand on. When boring a 1″ hole with a brace and bit (even a brace with a 10″ swing) it will be found that the job takes muscle. So the right working elevation will make it much easier to bore.

The lateral angle for brace alignment is represented by the straight line drawn from a marked hole center to a point on the center seat line (see brace direction drawing). Set a bevel gauge to 11° for a longitudinal or, if you will, front to back angle for the bit. There is a difference in front and back leg angles. The front legs are set on 11° and the back 19°. Place the pre-set bevel either over or parallel to the brace angle line drawn on seat. Start the bit in hole center mark, slanting the brace one way or the other to line it up laterally with the drawn line. Next, visually align the bit with the bevel. After every three or four turns, check both angles for accuracy. Repeat for the other front leg. Reset bevel for back legs and use the same procedure for the back postholes, changing only the bevel angle to 21°. While there is still a flat surface on the seat board, mark for five spindle holes to be bored 1/2″ diameter and 1″ deep. Use the same bevel angle as the posts and laterally line up the center with the center line. The first hole on either side of center, line up about 1″ to the side of center line. The second hole, line up to 2″ past center.

If your tools include a one inch #3 gouge it will be quicker to dish out the seat in the rough with that tool; otherwise your equipment should include a disc sander with a 1/4″ shaft to be used with a portable drill. Get some coarse- and fine-grit sanding discs. Use the coarse to dish out the seat in the rough.

Round the right-angle edges, top and bottom, as indicated on drawing. Rough- and finish-sand side edges and bottom. The top surface must be reworked after legs are glued in.

Turning is one operation that simply cannot be explained on paper. Put a leg blank in the lathe, pick up a big gouge, grit your teeth, and wade in. Seriously, make all lathe center marks as accurately as possible for a smooth, balanced spin. Turn leg-dowel endings to fit 1″ holes—post-dowels 7/8″.

When legs are turned, bore one 5/8″ hole in each where indicated for the front and back stretchers, judging a slight angle to counteract the leg rake. Set all four legs in place in the seat; measure for front and back stretchers. Add to that measurement 7/8″ and 7/8″ for a dowel at each end. Turn these two stretchers 7/8″ diameter with 5/8″ dowels on each end. Remove front legs. Insert stretcher; reset legs in seat; draw a pencil line around each dowel end on the top surface. These legs are not inter-changeable from now on. Remove the legs from seat, keeping each with its own hole. Saw off the excess dowel leaving about 1/8″ above the pencil line. Check the position of each leg in relation to seat grain direction; make a band-saw cut down the middle of each dowel holding the leg so the saw cut will be at right angle to seat grain direction. This cut continues to

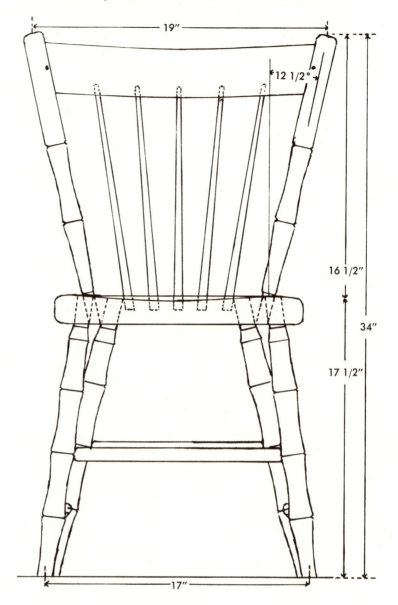

within 1/4″ of the shoulder indicating seat set position. Reassemble and reset in seat. Repeat in same sequence with back legs.

Now carefully mark for the side stretchers. Visually drawing a line from front to back leg, place pencil mark at what appears to be the center of the leg diameter viewing it from the other leg. Repeat from back to front leg. Repeat for the other side stretcher. Measure for stretchers where indicated on drawing. Add to the measurement between legs 3/4″ plus 1/2″ on

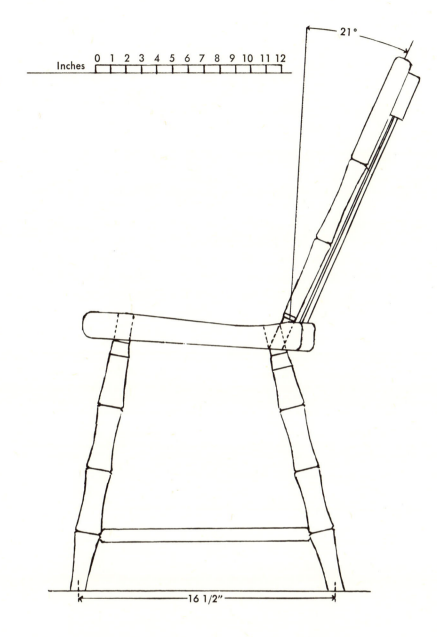

each end of each stretcher; the 1/2″ is to be removed after turning. Dowel ends are 5/8″ diameter and 3/4″ long.

Prepare 4 wedges of maple 1″ wide about 1 1/2″ long tapering from 1/4″ to nothing. Turn the seat upside down, remove the stretchers, placing them in positions easily identified as being for front, side, etc. Temporarily place each leg in its hole. Have enough room on one side of the seat which is on the worktable to assemble stretchers and legs before entering

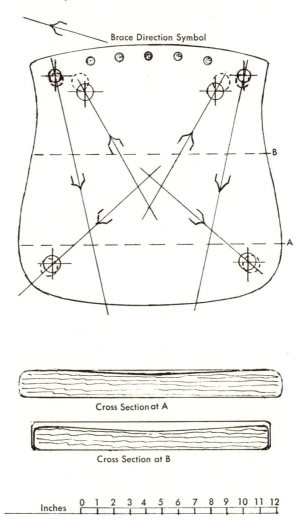

Brace Direction Symbol

Cross Section at A

Cross Section at B

Inches 0 1 2 3 4 5 6 7 8 9 10 11 12

seat holes. Remove one leg; coat stretcher hole with glue; enter stretcher; place this unit in its relative position to the seat. Remove the leg for the other end of stretcher #1; coat hole; enter stretcher. Now the right-angle stretcher for either leg—next the other stretcher and leg. That leaves, we will say, the back legs and back stretcher. Repeat with this assembly and coat the side holes with glue to complete the base structure. This gluing operation should be done as quickly as possible because each glued joint will probably have to be moved slightly when lining up the leg dowels to enter seat holes.

When you lift the seat plank to coat the holes with glue, remember the position so when it is replaced, it will not be turned one way or the

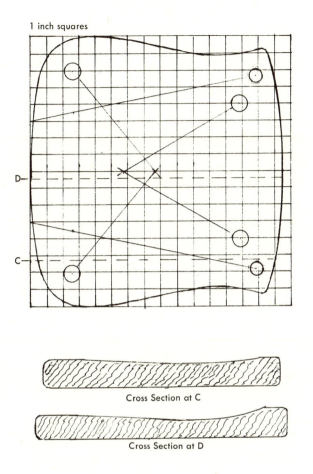

1 inch squares

D—

C—

Cross Section at C

Cross Section at D

other. Enter the leg dowels; tap in with a large hammer; be sure each leg is seated to an equal extent. Check each stretcher end to see that it is fully seated. Turn seat rightside up; coat a wedge on both sides with glue; enter it in a slot; quickly set it in tight with a large hammer. Repeat with 3 remaining legs. Allow overnight drying. Chisel off the protruding dowel and wedge wood. Resand the seat with coarse paper; carefully sand out all coarse scratches with a fine paper disc. Finally, a piece of 3/0 finishing paper covering a cork block should be used on the seat rubbing by hand with the grain. This eliminates even the fine circular scratches. Also sand the flat portion containing the back post and spindle holes.

Two back post blanks are needed—sized to 1 3/8″ × 1 3/8″ × 21 1/4″.

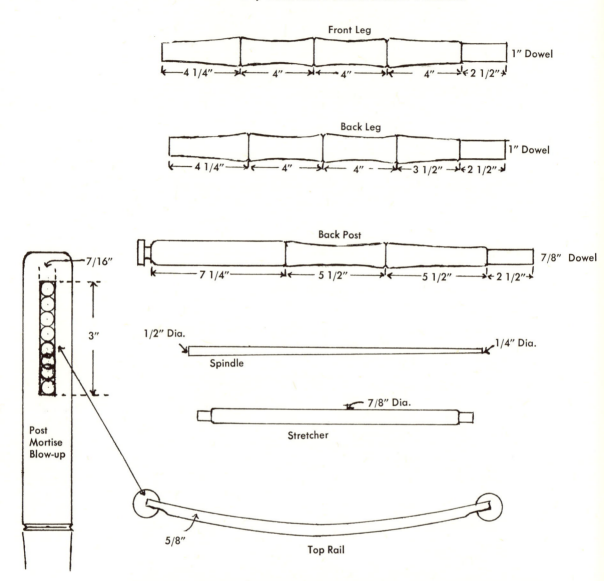

This length allows 1/2″ extra wood on the driving dog end to be sawed off after turning (observe the drawing). Insert the completed turnings in the seat holes; measure the post spread for sizing the poplar top rail. Mark 3/4″ down from the top of posts for start of rail mortise, then down 3″ more for the rail tenon. Accurately measure the distance between posts at the top marks. Add to that 7/8″ and 7/8″ for rail tenons. The drawing shows 12 1/2° off perpendicular which means that the crosscut gauge on the saw table will be set to that angle. The measurement made on the top mark is the longest; crosscut both ends.

Choose one side of the 1 3/4″ block for the face; set the circular saw to a depth of 7/8″ and the fence to cut 7/16″ width. Place the rail piece on end with face against the fence; pass over the saw; repeat on the other end. Now mark the radius which should take in all of the 1 3/4″ thickness. Leave 5/8″ between front and back lines; band-saw. On the tenon ends there remains a shoulder about 3/16″ to be removed. Use a curved gouge to do this job (check with drawing).

Observe post mortise blowup on drawing; between upper and lower marks, bore a line of 7/16″ holes 7/8″ deep. Straighten the walls with a 3/4″ chisel and square out the ends with a 1/4″ chisel; trial-fit rail tenons. Place assembly in seat holes—mark a pencil line around each post dowel where it comes through the seat bottom. Before disassembly, measure from seat to lower edge of rail; this will be the length of spindles plus 1″ into the seat and 3/4″ into the rail. Disassemble. Cut ends of dowels leaving 1/8″ over the pencil line. Make a band-saw slot in each dowel at right angle to rail mortise for wedge. Remove saw marks on rail, front and back, with a drawknife; finish-sand all four surfaces. Mark the lower edge for 5/16″ holes 3/4″ deep for 5 spindles, spacing them equidistant between posts and the spindles themselves.

Start with 5 spindle blanks 1/2″ × 1/2″ by the measured length. Set the jointer bed to a depth of 3/32″; place one side of a spindle down on the back bed so that the cutters will start tapering about 2″ from the end; pass over the cutters the full length; repeat on remaining 3 sides; repeat with all spindles. Use a small block plane to round the corners. Work them down until a reasonably round tapered spindle results. Sand first with coarse, then fine paper.

Coat the spindle holes in seat with glue; tap in the spindles. Now make a dry run (without glue) of the post and rail assembly to determine that the spindles are not too long. Should they hold the posts above seating position, remove the necessary wood to correct the error. Disassemble, coat the post mortises and rail tenons with glue; fit together; coat spindle holes in rail, post holes in seat with glue; insert the back assembly; tap to seat firmly; coat with glue and drive in post wedges.

Bore 3/16″ holes through the posts and rail ends for pins. Leave about 1/4″ of post wood from the drill to the rail. One pin in each rail end. Cut 2 pins about 1 1/2″ in length, coat hole with glue, and *quickly* drive in a pin before the glue catches and prevents the pin from going all the way through. Repeat. After overnight setting, chisel off the protruding post dowels, also the rail pins; finish-sand.

Now, stand back and take a long look. If you like what you see, pat yourself on the back because chairs are the most difficult pieces of furniture to make.

SUGGESTED STAIN MIX IS

> 5/8 Danish walnut
> 1/4 English oak
> 1/8 American cherry

·10·

Coffee Table

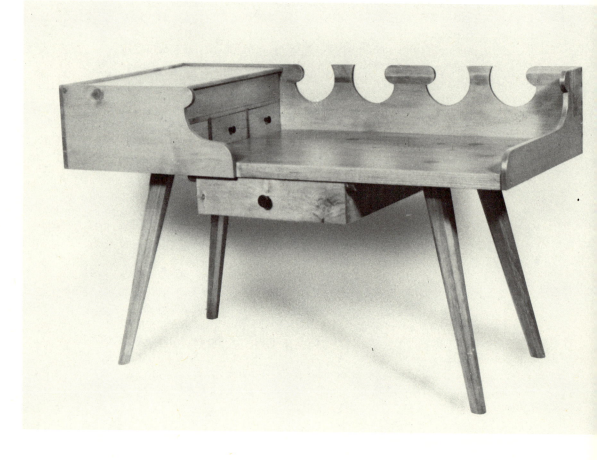

List of Materials

Rough measurements.

table top   41″ × 19″ × 1 1/8″ thick
leg blanks   (4)   20 1/4″ × 1 7/8″ × 1 7/8″
3/4″ wood for 3 case drawer fronts plus double-end drawer
    under top
1/2″ wood for superstructure
3/8″ wood for drawer sides, back, and bottoms
one-inch black knobs (2)
one-half-inch black knobs (3)

This table reminds one of a glorified cobbler's bench, unsuitable for a cobbler but extremely well designed for a living room. Knotty pine is the recommended wood.

Lumber dealers stock 1 1/4″ knotty pine that is already dressed to 1 1/16″ plus. This is the thickness for the top. The best plan would be to use 3 lengths of 8″ wide boards narrowing the center one to make up 18″ in width. Glue together for a top 18″ wide × 41″ (rough) long. After overnight setting, square the ends to 40″ finish size.

Bore leg holes next. Set a bevel gauge to 8°. Mark the top, as indicated on drawing, 7 3/8″ from end and 4″ in from the side. Do this on each corner. Place the bevel on the top, lining it with the brace direction line; bore a 1 1/4″ hole through the top carefully keeping the brace lined up vertically with bevel also in line with the brace direction line on drawing. Repeat for all 4 holes.

Finish-size 4 leg pieces, 19 1/4″ × 1 7/8″ × 1 7/8″. Center-mark the ends of each piece for lathe mounting. Turn a 1 1/4″ diameter dowel 2″ long on one end of each piece. Instead of a square shoulder at the dowel end, angle the cut as shown on drawing. To taper the legs, set the jointer bed for a depth of 3/16″. Lower a leg onto the back bed up close to the turned dowel—this will result in a tapered cut starting at nothing and ending at the bottom end 3/16″ deep. Repeat one more cut on the same surface; three more right angle surfaces done the same way will complete one leg. Do the remaining 3 legs in like manner. Angle the jointer fence to 45°; set front bed to cut a depth of 3/16″; pass each right angle corner over the jointer for the entire leg length. Repeat with remaining three legs. Cut a band-saw slot down the center of each dowel end (width of saw blade)

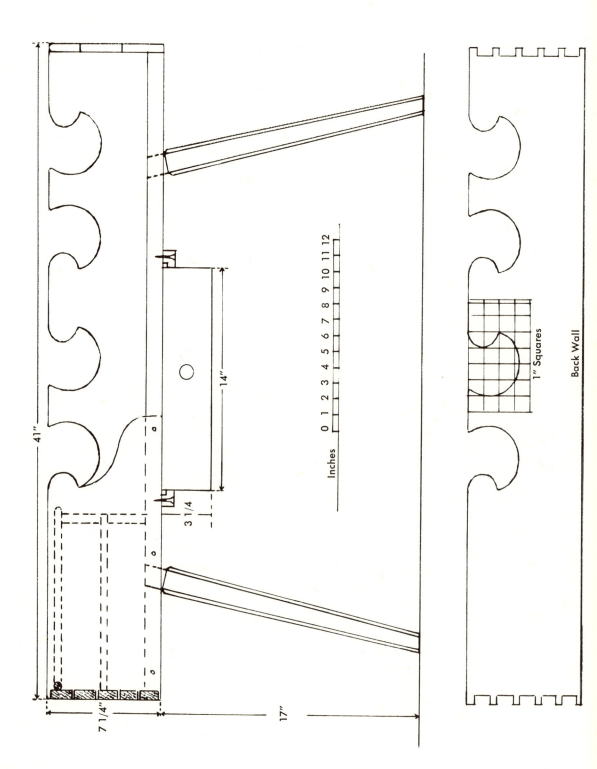

41"

7 1/4"

17"

3 1/4

14"

Inches

0 1 2 3 4 5 6 7 8 9 10 11 12

1" Squares

Back Wall

at right angle to a leg surface. This will complete the millwork on the legs. Finish-sand all leg surfaces except dowels.

Determine how much sanding you wish to do to the under side of top. Complete that work. Coat a leg hole with glue, insert a leg dowel keeping the slot at right angle to the grain direction of top wood. Have prepared, beforehand, wedges about 1 1/2" long by 1 1/4" wide with a taper of about 1/4". Coat with glue one of these wedges; insert in the slot; seat solidly with a large hammer. Repeat with 3 remaining legs. After overnight glue hardening, remove the extra dowel wood with a chisel and mallet. At this time, just rough-sand the top.

Milling the wall pieces above the top should be done next. Enough 1/2" wood provided can be ripped to 7 1/4". Square-cut the back wall to exactly one inch longer than the table top. Square the left case end exactly one inch longer than the top width. Square the right wall 1/2" longer than the top width. The short front wall at the case end should be squared to 17 1/2". The compartment bottom must be glued to provide a panel the length of which can be determined by the width of tabletop plus 1/8" and 1/8" tongues. The width of this panel is 12". The lift lid can also be glued at this time. The finished size is length 1" plus width of top, its width is 12 1/2". After rough-sanding, size the compartment bottom to length, 1/4" plus top width and 12" wide.

Study the case cross section on drawing; thoroughly understand what you wish to accomplish next. Grooves must be provided for division members and the compartment bottom. Set up the 1/2" dado to cut to a depth of 1/8". On the table end chosen for the case work, divide the width into 3 equal parts allowing for 2 one-half inch thick division pieces. Set the fence to cut on these measured marks; the setting will serve for both grooves, one from each side. Grooves are to be 12" long. Adjust fence to compensate for 1/4" extra width (length of wood) of compartment bottom so grooves run on this piece will match (in perpendicular) the ones on tabletop.

The back and front walls will need supporting grooves for the compartment bottom which also serves as the top board for case drawers. Set the fence for these grooves to exact thickness of tabletop plus 2 1/2". Cut grooves in length to 12" for drawer plus 1/2" for end wall. Remember that these wall pieces may already have had one end chosen for case end, so grooves will be cut as a pair. The grooves cut in front and back walls plus those run on tabletop should have the measured length end squared out with hand tools so the 1/2" thick pieces inserted will come up even with the intended length. The grooves run on the under side of compartment bottom are cut through the entire width of wood so there are no blind endings to square out.

The front, back, and right end walls may now be laid off in one-inch squares where indicated on drawing for band-saw work. After sawing, slightly round the top straight edge on all four walls with hand tools;

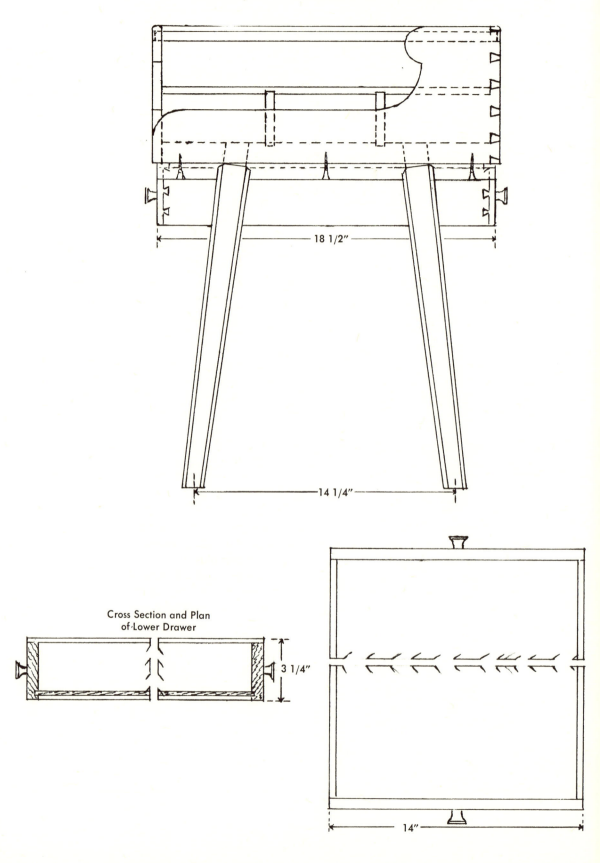

Cross Section and Plan
of Lower Drawer

3 1/4"

18 1/2"

14 1/4"

14"

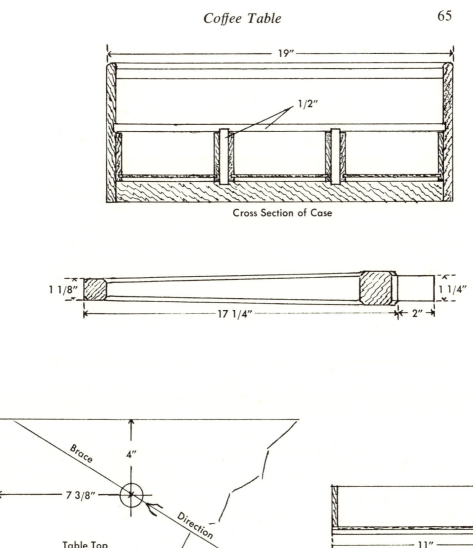

Cross Section of Case

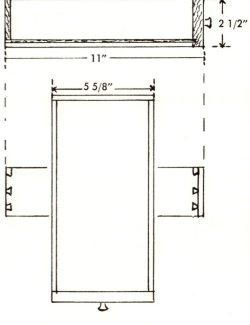

Cross Section and Plan
of Case Drawers

smooth out with sandpaper all handsawed marks on curved edges; finish-sand all inside surfaces. Dovetailing is illustrated adequately on drawing; the only difference between these walls and an average drawer is that all four pieces are 1/2″ thick—which means that the dovetailing is the full wood thickness, eliminating what is normally a thicker drawer front. Finish-sand the inside surfaces of the walls.

The last panel to be worked on is the compartment lid. Study the drawing; it can be observed that left and right edges (width of panel) are formed into a half round. The length of panel is the exact width of top plus 1/2″ and 1/2″ for thickness of front and back walls. This measurement allows for a 1/2″ long dowel on each end to serve as a hinge for the lift lid. To form these dowel extensions, set the bench saw to cut away 1/2″ of wood on each end of panel but only up to the dowel extension; finish rounding dowels with hand tools. Finish-sand lid all around. Bore 1/2″ receiving holes in front and back walls where indicated for dowels of lift lid.

The remaining 1/2″ thick members to be milled are the two drawer divisions and the compartment end riser. The drawer openings are milled for 2 1/2″ height so the dividers must be 2 1/2″ plus 1/8″ top and 1/8″ bottom, exactly 12″ long. The last compartment wallpiece should be sawed to 2 3/8″ wide. That measurement is determined by adding 2 1/2″ drawer, 1/2″ compartment bottom, 1/4″ above lift lid, and 1/2″ lid; the difference is 2 3/8″. The length of this piece is to be exactly the width of tabletop. Finish-sand at this time.

In case sanding instructions were omitted for any part, all surfaces of all parts are to be finish-sanded at this time, except the outside surfaces of the 4 walls.

The superstructure assembly may now be done. Lay the back wall on worktable (inside surface up). Coat the dovetails of left wall, both ends, with glue; insert tails into back openings; place compartment bottom in grooves provided; insert lift lid dowel in hole bored in back wall; line up front wall openings with tails cut into left wall; press into place, using a rubber mallet for a tight seat. Now the right wall tails may be coated with glue and inserted into the back wall. This assembly should be a snug fit when placed over the tabletop. Allow overnight hardening before attachment.

Place 2 drawer division pieces in grooves provided in tabletop, position superstructure assembly, and press down to the point where the bottom edge is flush with the bottom of the tabletop. Span the assembly from front to back with a bar clamp to keep both parts in position. Provide 3/16″ dowels about 1 1/2″ long; bore three 3/16″ holes through the front wall into the tabletop, slanting them as you would driving a toe nail. Coat the holes with glue, drive in dowels. Repeat on back wall (about five dowels) then the two ends (three dowels).

Position the remaining compartment wall above the drawer openings, holding firmly in place using a bar clamp from front to back; carefully bore two 3/16″ holes (toed in) through the front into the wall; glue and seat dowels. Repeat on back wall. After glue hardening, all protruding dowel ends may be chiseled off and all 4 walls rough- and finish-sanded.

The three case drawers are nothing special so carefully follow the instructions in the chapter on dovetailing. It is suggested that you use 5/16″ thick wood for sides, backs, and bottoms and 5/8″ wood for fronts.

The hanging drawer underneath is special because it is made with two fronts; it can be pulled from front or back. This means that the bottom board must be cut accurately to fit into all 4 grooves, 2 fronts and 2 sides, before assembly. We suggest, when making a drawer this size, the side wood should be 3/8″ thick, bottom board only 5/16″, and the two fronts 3/4″ thick. After assembly, finish-sand the completed drawer; glue and brad a 1/4″ × 1/4″ strip along the top edge of each side piece. Consult the drawing for these strips and the drawer runners in which they slide.

THE STAIN MIXTURE FOR PINE IS

3/4 English oak
1/8 Danish walnut
1/8 American cherry

•11•

Trestle Table

LIST OF MATERIALS

Rough measurements.

top		3/4″ thick × 18″ wide × 27″ long
skirting	(2 sides)	3/4″ thick × 3 1/2″ wide × 27″ long
skirting	(2 ends)	3/4″ thick × 3 1/2″ wide × 16″ long
foot	(2)	3/4″ thick × 3 1/2″ wide × 16″ long
vertical ends	(2)	3/4″ thick × 6″ wide × 22″ long
trestle bar		1 1/8″ thick × 3 1/2″ wide × 27″ long

This table should not be overlooked when planning an Early American room. Its contribution to the desired atmosphere is most important, especially when it is made of knotty pine.

Under the discussion of woods you will recall that #2 white pine (knotty pine) can be procured in the desired thicknesses from any lumber dealer —large or small.

Start work on the skirt pieces—since the feet and skirt ends are the same size, include the feet when sizing the skirt parts. We will refer to the long pieces as sides because, being both alike, they are not, strictly speaking, front and back. Saw to 3″ widths two side skirts, two end skirts, and two foot pieces. Square-cut the sides to 22″ length, the ends and footers to 15 1/4″ length.

Next, saw the end supports to 5 1/2″ width. Square-cut these two pieces to 21 1/4″. Mill 1/4″ tenons on the four ends by placing on the saw-arbor two dado side cutters with a 1/4″ spacer between. Raise the arbor to cut a depth of 3/4″. Set the fence to place the tenon in the center of the 3/4″ wood thickness. That will divide 3/4″ wood into three equal parts—1/4″ shoulder on each side surface and a 1/4″ tenon in the center. Pass each end of these pieces over the dado assembly, end up, pressing the wood surface against the fence. Replace the dado setup with a saw blade. Set fence for a 3/4″ cut, including saw blade. Set the saw for 1/4″ depth of cut. Pass each side surface of each end over the saw to form the necessary shoulders. While keeping the fence setup, raise the saw blade to cut a depth of 1/2″. In conjunction with the fence setting, adjust crosscut gauge to 90°, edge-up each support piece, holding it against crosscut gauge

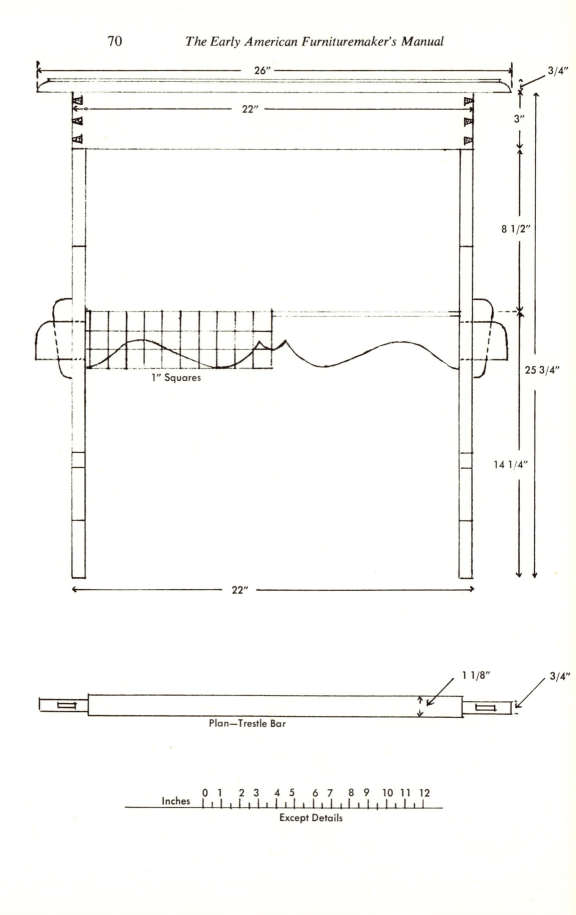

26"

3/4"

22"

3"

8 1/2"

1" Squares

25 3/4"

14 1/4"

22"

1 1/8"

3/4"

Plan—Trestle Bar

Inches   0 1   2 3   4 5   6 7   8 9   10 11 12

Except Details

with the end pressed to the fence; pass over the saw. Repeat on eight edges. Readjust fence to cut 1/2″ including blade; raise saw to cut a depth of 3/4″. Place support pieces end up side surface against crosscut gauge pressing edge against fence; pass over saw. Repeat to finish-cut eight tenon edge shoulders.

Chuck a 1/4″ drill in the press; clamp a back fence on the press table in a position for the drill to bore a line of holes intended for each mortise in the center of 3/4″ wood thickness. On your choice for the top edges of foot pieces and bottom edges of end skirts, measure and mark 2 1/4″ from the center toward each end. Make the drill setting for a depth of 13/16″ into 3″ high wood. Hold end skirt and foot pieces in turn firmly against the fence; bore between the 4 1/2″ spaced marks hole to hole (see mortise detail on drawing).

Next, saw shoulders on side and end skirt pieces. The method shown on drawing (milling detail) provides a good seating shoulder plus reducing the dovetail wood to a more convenient thickness. On both ends of the side skirt pieces, cut away 1/4″ of wood leaving 1/2″ thickness. The shoulder line is 3/4″ from the end allowing the milled end skirt to seat firmly when dovetails are cut. Shoulders on end pieces leave 1/2″ wood thickness, but only 1/2″ in from the end instead of the 3/4″ provided on side pieces.

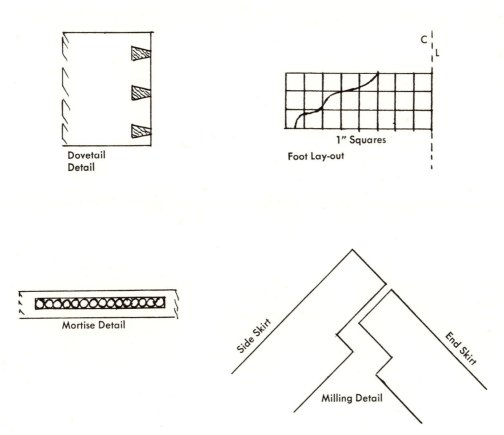

Dovetail
Detail

1″ Squares

Foot Lay-out

Mortise Detail

Side Skirt

End Skirt

Milling Detail

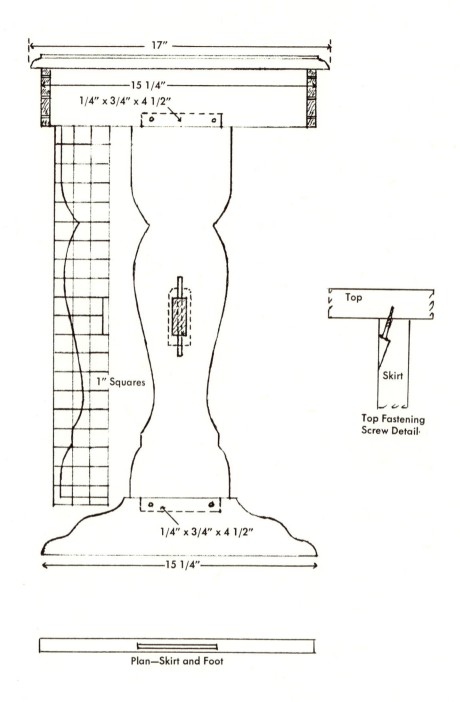

17"

15 1/4"

1/4" x 3/4" x 4 1/2"

1" Squares

1/4" x 3/4" x 4 1/2"

15 1/4"

Top

Skirt

Top Fastening
Screw Detail·

Plan—Skirt and Foot

Dovetails may now be cut. We will use the chapter on dovetailing as a guide. The end skirts can be compared to the drawer front illustrated except that the tails are laid off for full 1/2" wood thickness (not blind as done on drawer fronts). Side skirts are cut exactly like drawer sides.

Make a pattern for the foot members by following the foot layout on drawing. Band-saw and sand sawed edges. Follow the same procedure for end supports—make pattern, band-saw, and sand edges. The trestle ends may now be assembled. Coat the mortise walls of a skirt and a foot piece with glue, also glue the tenons on one of the support pieces. When assembling the end unit, be sure the skirt piece is fitted to the top of the support. When assembled with hand pressure, place in a bar clamp and draw up tight. Repeat for the other end assembly. After overnight drying, it will be more convenient to sand (coarse and fine) the two end units before further assembly.

Now the trestle bar may be milled. Start with a piece 1 1/8" thick by 3" wide by 26" long. Shoulders are to be cut on the ends leaving exactly 20 1/2" between cuts. Use the tenon procedure described for end supports. Cut away enough waste wood for a resulting tenon-like end that measures 2 3/4" long by 7/8" thick by 2" wide or high. Since dado side cutters will not cut to a depth of 2 3/4", a circular saw must be used. Set the saw to the required height; set the fence close to the saw blade so only 1/8" of wood will be removed. Hold the bar end up with its side against the fence; pass over the saw; repeat with the other side of the same end, then two cuts on the other end. Top and bottom shoulders are milled by following tenon instructions.

Holes must be provided in the end supports for trestle bar insertion.

Lay out the holes, 7/8" wide × 2" high, position as shown on drawing. Make cutouts with the jigsaw.

A tapered slot must be bored, then cleaned out with chisels through the trestle bar ends. Lay off these 1/4" holes in the center of the 7/8" width. The slots will start 5/8" from shoulders and end 1 3/4" from shoulders; these are measurements for the top. The bottom opening should be measured from the shoulders 5/8" and 1 1/2". When slots are prepared, insert bar into end supports and make tapered wedges to fit snugly. All details are illustrated on drawing. The last detail on bar ends is to saw a 1" radius on the top corners. Finish-sand the entire bar. The two side skirt pieces may now be attached to end units. Coat the walls of all tails with glue, enter and seat the trestle bar in both ends; lay this assembly on its side and position a side member; tap in place with either a rubber mallet or a hammer and block. Turn on the other side and repeat with the second side rail.

Glue edge to edge the boards provided for the top, making a panel about 27" long by 18" wide. After overnight setting in bar clamps, saw to finish-width (17") and square the ends to a finish-size of 26".

Rough-sand both top and bottom surfaces of the top panel. A thumbnail molding may now be cut on all four edges. If a shaper is not available, the 1/8″ deep shoulder 1/2″ in from the edge will be done best on the circular saw. Raise the blade to cut 1/2″ high. Set the fence 1/8″ less than the thickness of the top panel. Edge up the panel, press against fence, and pass over saw on all four sides. Use a small block plane to round the remaining right-angle corner. Coarse- and fine-sand molding; finish-sand top surface.

Observe the top fastening screw detail on drawing. About 3″ in from the corner on all four skirt pieces, bore a screw clearance hole 11/64″ on an angle. About 3/4″ from the top of skirt edge, cut a shoulder around the screw hole to provide a seat for 1 1/4″ #7 screws. On the long side pieces a center screw hole may be bored.

Place top, unside down, on a worktable, position table base accurately on top, clamp in two places to prevent shifting, and seat all ten screws.

THE STAIN MIXTURE FOR PINE IS

    3/4 English oak
    1/8 Danish walnut
    1/8 American cherry

·12·

Dining Table

LIST OF MATERIALS

board   1 1/4″ × 12″ × 8′
board   1 1/4″ × 12″ × 10′
boards (2)   1″ × 6″ × 8′
piece for legs 2″ × 9″ × 30″ long
12″ ball-bearing turntable

This table was chosen because it is so well suited to the Early American theme which governed previous selections. Pine is the ideal wood for this design.

The material list has two boards 1 1/4″ thick. That thickness is in the rough and on which the price is based. The lumberyard has this thickness already planed to 1 1/8″ and in most lengths and widths. Two 1″ boards are also listed—as previously noted, these are in stock dressed to 3/4″.

The 2″ × 9″ × 30″ long should be in the rough when purchased because as much thickness as possible should be retained for leg blanks. Rip 4 leg squares 2″ × 2″ out of this piece; pass over the jointer, 2 right-angle sides of each piece just deep enough to clear saw cut marks. Set circular saw fence to cut just enough to result in a uniform width; the drawing calls for 1 15/16″ square but it is possible that only 1 7/8″ can be realized. The two remaining sawed sides of each piece should be jointed lightly. Cut all four leg blanks to 28 1/4″ finished length.

These legs are offset turnings—that means the lathe center markings are critical. Make sure you understand the position of marks on the drawing before proceeding. It is well to point out that after marking one end, the leg may be moved to a more convenient position, but *do not* rotate it to any of the other three sides. Keep the same side facing you as when marking the first end. Mark second end as shown; repeat with remaining legs. Please observe that the top end is marked directly opposite to the foot. The dotted line running through the leg drawing represents the turning center when mounted correctly. It may also be noted that at point 5 3/4″ down (where the square portion ends and turning begins), the dotted line is centered on the leg blank. The top mark throws that end slightly off center in the opposite direction to the foot marking which is proportionately farther off-set. It will be necessary to slow the lathe rpm because of off balance; after the leg is turned to an approximate round, speed may be increased.

As shown on drawing and photo, turning starts 5 3/4″ down from top

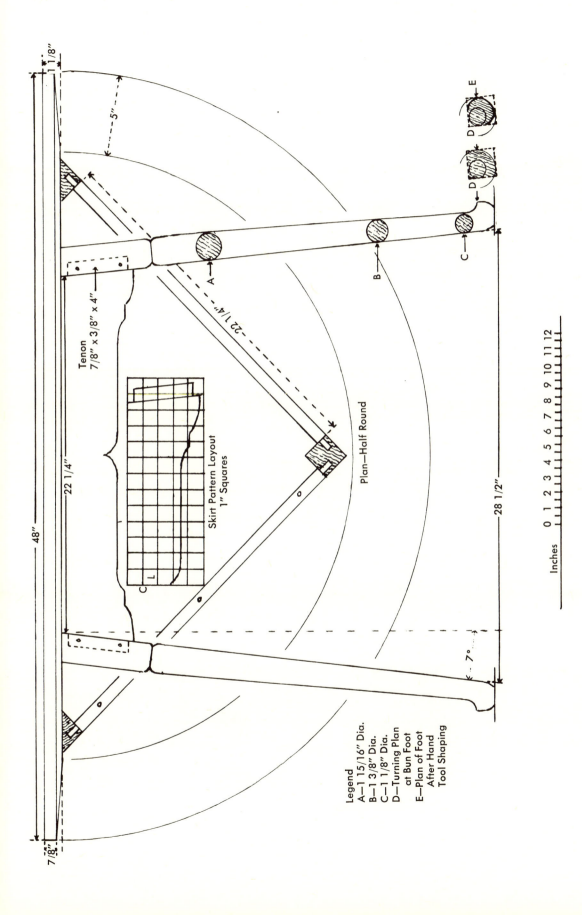

1 1/8"

5"

Tenon
7/8" x 3/8" x 4"

22 1/4"

A

B

C

Plan—Half Round

Skirt Pattern Layout
1" Squares

C

L

48"

22 1/4"

7/8"

28 1/2"

7°

D

D

E

Legend
A—1 15/16" Dia.
B—1 3/8" Dia.
C—1 1/8" Dia.
D—Turning Plan
     at Bun Foot
E—Plan of Foot
     After Hand
     Tool Shaping

Inches   0 1 2 3 4 5 6 7 8 9 10 11 12

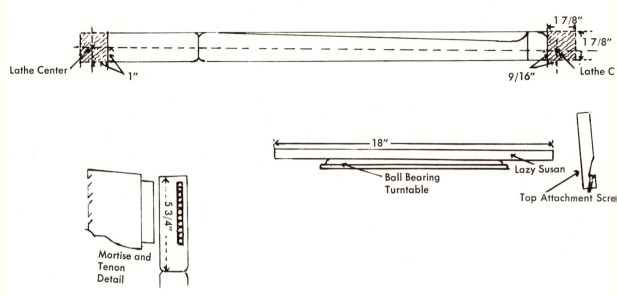

Lathe Center   1"   1 7/8"   1 7/8"   9/16"   Lathe C

18"   Ball Bearing Turntable   Lazy Susan   Top Attachment Scre

Mortise and Tenon Detail   5 3/4"

and stops at point D on drawing (leaving about 1 1/8" unturned). The foot will be worked down with hand tools in the following manner: Looking down on the foot from the top you see three corners of the square; the center one is called the front corner. Draw a line (freehand) to closely follow Figure E, still looking down on the foot. Now, before attempting to lessen the diameter as it reaches the floor, use a sharp chisel (about 3/4") to remove the wood to the pencil line keeping about the same size and shape at the bottom. Now rounding can be done as indicated on drawing to about 1 1/4" at the bottom; round also the short square section on the back corner; finish-sand the hand-tool work; hand-tool the other three legs.

Saw 4 skirt pieces 4 3/4" × 26 1/4" rough length from 3/4" lumber. Set the crosscut gauge to 7° off right angle; crosscut one end of each piece; clamp a stop block on crosscut fence to cut a finish length (on the top edge) of 24 1/4" plus 7/8" and 7/8" for tenons; make the second cuts. Set up dado side cutters with 3/8" spacer between, 7/8" depth of cut; adjust ripping fence to cut a 5/16" shoulder on the face side; pass all skirt ends over this setup; put combination saw blade back on mandrel; set fence to cut 7/8" long tenons with front shoulders of 5/16" and 1/16" on the backs. Now cut 3/8" of wood from tenon tops and bottoms (mortise and tenon detail).

Follow skirt pattern layout for marking and band-sawing the skirt pieces. Only one half of one skirt piece need be laid off in one-inch squares. When that section is sawed, use it for a pattern on the other pieces; sand band-sawed edges reasonably smooth.

Mark the two leg sides which form the inside back corner to prevent an error when mortising for tenons. Mark in the mortising area 3/8" and

4 3/8″ down from leg top; this is the length of mortise. Chuck a 3/8″ bit in the drill press; set fence to leave 5/16″ of wood to the front corner; set bit stop to a depth of 15/16″. This next is important: When boring a series of holes in line for mortise, be sure that one front face is down on the press table and the other right-angle face is against the fence. It will be necessary to turn the leg end for end to bore for the other mortise; repeat with remaining legs.

Using a 3/4″ chisel, chop the long mortise walls to a straight line; use a 1/4″ chisel to square out the ends and clean out the bottom; repeat with three more legs; finish-sand all mortised surfaces.

Glue and bar-clamp first one skirt with a leg on each end (naturally keeping the right-angle mortises pointing inward). Glue and clamp a second skirt in the same manner. Glue the four remaining mortises and tenons; assemble as a 4-sided unit spanning the two remaining sides with bar clamps (clamping on the first clamps); shift clamps if necessary to bring unit into square. After overnight setting, bore two 3/16″ holes as indicated on drawing in each joint for pins. Cut, glue, and drive in pins; after glue-hardening, chisel off protruding pins, rough- and fine-sand outside surfaces of skirts and legs (which should be flush with each other).

Because of the rake angle, the extreme front leg corners will be slightly higher than the skirt line; either chisel or sand down these points to get a uniform straight line for top attachment; three holes for #8 screws in each skirt for top fastening (see drawing).

Cut 1 1/8″ top boards to rough length (2 strips off the extra two feet will be needed to fill out the 48″ width). Before gluing, play safe by passing all board edges over the jointer to be sure of good clean, square joint edges. Should the lack of sufficiently long bar clamps pose a problem, your lumber dealer will glue this top for you.

Use a trammel to pencil in a 48″ circle line—have help available to hold up table top when band-sawing. Remove saw marks with draw knife; finish-sand edge. Rough-sand table top; set scratch gauge and mark the edge 7/8″ down from the top; set the hand plane to cut rather deeply and plane a long taper from 5″ in to the 7/8″ thick line on the edge (see drawing). Finish-sand this tapered surface. Attach base to top with 1 1/2″ #8 screws. Finish-sand top surface.

Glue together 3/4″ boards for an 18″ lazy susan top; band-saw the circle; draw-knife the edge; rough-sand top and bottom surfaces. Because of its design, should it be necessary to fasten the turntable to the top board with screws down from the top surface, counterbore, fasten, and plug the screws before finish-sanding the top surface.

STAIN MIX FOR PINE IS

   3/4 English oak
   1/8 Danish walnut
   1/8 American cherry

·13·

Occasional Table

List of Materials

Rough length except leg blanks.

legs	(4)	1 7/8″ × 1 7/8″ × 26 3/8″ long
top		21″ long × 20″ wide × 5/8″ thick
side and back panels	(3)	16 1/2″ long × 9″ wide × 3/4″ thick
front drawer dividers	(3)	16 1/2″ long × 1 7/8″ wide × 3/4″ thick
drawer fronts	(2)	15 1/2″ long × 3 1/2″ wide × 5/8″ thick
3/8″ poplar for drawer sides, backs, and bottoms		
pine or poplar for drawer runners		1 3/4″ × 1 3/4″ × about 48″ long
1″ brushed-brass knobs	(4)	

This table was made especially to be photographed for this book. It has a figured maple top and drawer fronts with the frame of cherry. Using a combination of two woods was not uncommon in the old days. The table would still be an attractive piece if it were made entirely of maple, cherry, walnut, or even pine.

To start the table, the leg blanks should be turned. These turnings are not a particularly difficult design. After marking the centers and mounting in the lathe, measure down from the top end 10″ and mark on 2 of the four sides so it will be visible when spinning. That 10″ is the portion of leg left unturned—check with the drawing blowup for diameters and length measurements.

Because the table is square, the front, side, and back members are the same length—14 1/2″ plus 1/2″ and 1/2″ for tongues on the side and back panels and the same extensions for all front dovetails. Two side and one back panel are to be finished sized to 15 1/2″ long × 9″ wide × 3/4″ thick. The front pieces are finished to 15 1/2″ × 1 7/8″ wide × 3/4″ thick.

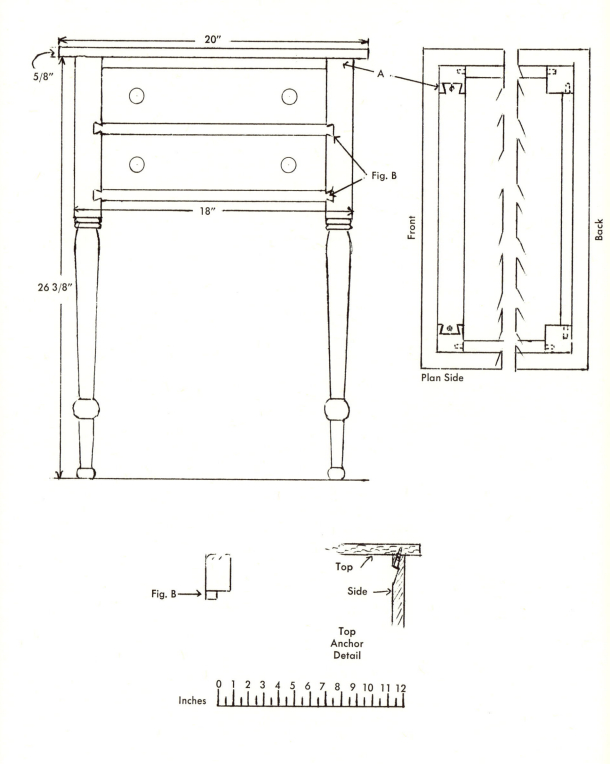

Front

Back

Plan Side

A

Fig. B

20"

5/8"

18"

26 3/8"

Fig. B →

Top

Side →

Top
Anchor
Detail

Inches   0 1 2 3 4 5 6 7 8 9 10 11 12

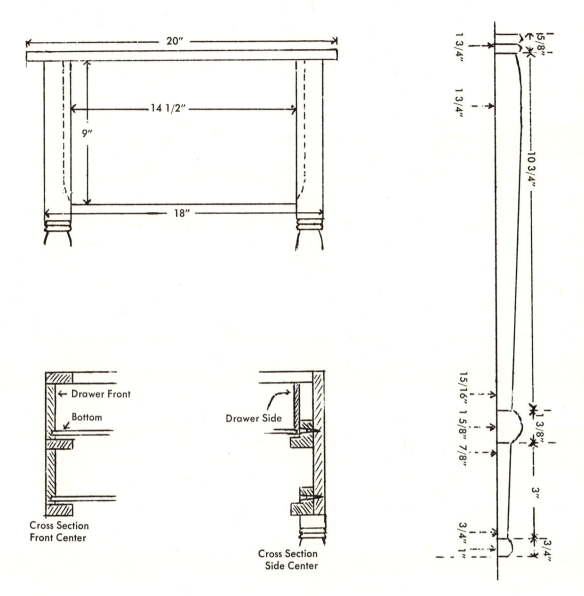

Cut tongues on the side and back panels before measuring for grooves in legs. Set up the dado side cutters with a 1/4" spacer between; raise to cut 1/2" in height. Set the fence to leave a 5/16" shoulder on the outside face; pass the ends of all three panels over the dado holding the face against the fence. Milling on the front pieces will be done with a combination saw instead of the dado; replace the dado with a saw blade, setting it so as to cut 1/2″ wide and 5/16″ high. Pass all tongued ends (face down) over this setup. Lower saw to 3/16″ for back shoulder cut. Replace the saw blade with the two side dado cutters to mill the 1/4″ grooves in legs. Space the fence setting to match exactly the outside shoulder on side panel tongue; raise dado to cut a depth or height of nearly 9/16″. Now group the four legs (standing upright) to make a square; pencil-mark on leg top where each groove is to be milled on each leg; now each leg will have its own corner and not be interchangeable. Half of the grooves will be milled by passing legs over the dado starting at the top with the groove not to exceed 8 3/4″ in length. The remaining grooves will be cut by lowering the leg onto the saw table at a premarked point to result in a groove 8 3/4″ long.

Before milling the ends of front pieces, be sure you understand what is to be accomplished. The top strip will have a shoulder cut on the bottom surface, measured to leave a 1/2″ extension 1 7/8″ wide × 1/4″ thick (plan—Fig. A). It is unnecessary to chop into the top of legs to a depth of 3/4″. After band-sawing the dovetail shape, position the piece on top of a front leg; scribe an outline of the tail; mark this strip end and the leg for correct assembly later. Repeat with the other strip end and leg. Dovetailing procedure is exactly the same as for drawer fronts, chopping into the leg top to a depth equal to the tail thickness.

The middle and lower strips will have the dovetails set in from front to back (see drawing and photo). Again, it is unnecessary to have the tail go all the way back. 3/4″ deep will be sufficient (Fig. B). To mill for these pieces, set the saw to cut a 1/2″ extension and to a depth of 1 1/8″ from back to front; hold a strip with the back edge on the table and against the squared crosscut gauge; make this cut on all four ends. Now make the other right-angle setup by placing the fence to leave 3/4″ from front to back, a depth of 1/2″. Hold a strip on end; face edge against fence, steadying it against the crosscut gauge; pass over saw; repeat with other ends. To shape the dovetail, place the back edge on the band-saw table; mark freehand the angled sides to give it the tail shape; saw to lines. Repeat.

The lower strip is placed on the front surface of a front leg (be sure the groove for side panel is positioned correctly) 9″ down from leg top; scribe outline, mark strip for later matching. Repeat other end. The middle strip is placed so each drawer opening is equal in height; scribe, mark for matching; repeat.

Your shop equipment should have a small fine-toothed back saw. If not, one may be purchased at any hobby shop. Use this saw to carefully follow the tail angle lines; it will be well to mark squared pencil lines on the drawer-side surface of the leg being worked on. If the saw cut should nearly reach the back corner of the leg surface before tailing out, no harm is done. There is a choice now in method used for removing waste wood. It may be removed entirely with a small chisel or the largest permissible bit can be used, boring in the drawer-side surface to a depth of 1/2″; now use the small chisel to straighten lines and clean out corners. Repeat with remaining three cutouts; try fitting each before assembly. The 1/4″ leg grooves for side and back panels do not have to be squared out to depth at the bottom. As is shown by dotted lines on drawing, the tongues can be band-sawed to follow these radii.

Because of the three cross members that make up the front it will be well to glue this unit first. Coat the cavities and tails with glue; tap into place, seat a one-inch nail in each end of the top piece; span the assembly at the center division with a bar clamp and draw tight. Coat the back tongues and grooves with glue; enter tongues (keeping top edge of panel even with top of legs), span with a bar clamp about center, and draw tight. Use the same procedure for each side; the only difference will be that the clamps will pull against the front and back ones already in use. Angle the last two clamps slightly, if necessary, to bring the case into square.

All outside surfaces may now be coarse- and fine-sanded. Should there be any joint that shows one member to be raised too much above the adjoining one for sanding, take it down flush with a sharp plane before sanding.

Drawing cross sections show what must be done to support the drawers. The distance from side panel inside surface and the inside corner of a leg should be about 1 1/8″. The list of materials calls for a piece of pine 1 3/4″ × 1 3/4″ for this purpose. Before milling, cut four pieces to fit between front and back legs. The top inside corners of these pieces will be cut out leaving 1 1/8″ of wood for a side wall and 3/4″ (the thickness of front division piece) for the drawer to slide on. There is also another reason for this bottom to measure 3/4″—the bottom of the support block is flush with the bottom of center division piece which will prevent the lower drawer from rocking up and down when slid about halfway out. Bore two 11/64″ screw holes in each piece; countersink so drawers will slide past the screw heads. Position and fasten as indicated on drawing.

Slope two 11/64″ screw holes in each side and the back panel for top attachment (see top anchor detail). Also two holes can be bored through the front top strip; angle them slightly so screwdriver will clear the center division strip; countersink so drawer will not scrape.

There is nothing special about the two drawers, so the chapter on dovetailing can be followed—5/8″ drawer fronts and 3/8″ poplar for sides, backs, and bottoms.

Prepare the tabletop by gluing together enough 21″ long × 5/8″ thick boards to make up 20″ wide; after setting, square to size 20″ × 20″; edges are left square; remove all saw marks with coarse and fine sandpaper. Rough-sand bottom and top panel; first rough- then fine-sand top surface. Place the top (upside down) on worktable, the frame placed with an even margin all around; clamp to hold in place; sink anchor screws in on all four sides. To keep the top drawer from rocking, screw a fill-in strip 3/4″ × about one inch near center from front to back.

If maple and cherry have been used to make this table, the following stain mixes can be applied.

FOR MAPLE USE THE PINE MIX

> 3/4 English oak
> 1/8 Danish walnut
> 1/8 American cherry

FOR BETTER CONTRAST, STAIN THE CHERRY WITH THIS MIX

> 7/8 Danish walnut
> 1/8 American cherry

and, to about 1 pint of the mixture, add 3 teaspoonsful of Vandyke Brown color in oil.

·14·

Bedside Table
Circa 1750

LIST OF MATERIALS

Rough measurements except leg blanks.

top   20″ × 20″ × 5/8″ thick
legs   (4)   1 9/16″ × 1 9/16″ × 27 7/8″ long
skirting (2 sides)   17″ × 4 1/2″ × 3/4″ thick
skirting   (back)   17″ × 4 1/2″ × 3/4″ thick
front strips   (2)   17″ × 1 5/8″ × 5/8″ thick
drawer front   15″ × 3 1/4″ × 3/4″ thick
3/8″ thick poplar to make drawer sides, back and bottom
1″ brushed-brass round knob for drawer pull

We call this a bedside table although it is equally at home in the living room, den, or entrance hall.

The wood used can be walnut, cherry, maple, or possibly pine. Because of the comparatively thin top (5/8″), pine is not recommended.

Start with the leg blanks. They should be 1 9/16″ × 1 9/16″ × 27 7/8″ long. This is another table that calls for the leg taper to be worked on the right angle inside surfaces only. To accomplish this operation, place a starting mark on the back jointer bed, measured to allow the jointer knives to start cutting 5 1/4″ down from the top end when the leg piece is held on mark and lowered. The number of cuts will depend upon the depth of each cut. The finished size called for is 7/8″ × 7/8″. Mark each surface that has been tapered; these are the sides that will be mortised for skirting.

It is customary to size and tenon skirt pieces before mortising because it is less difficult to accurately match the mortise to the tenon shoulder.

The two side and one back skirt pieces are the same size. The two front strips, being the same length as the sides and back, should be squared to length with the other pieces. Allowing 3/4″ for the length of each tenon, the skirt pieces should be cut to 16 1/8″. The two sides and back are to be 4 1/4″ wide. The front strips, above and below the drawer opening, should measure 16 1/8″ × 1 9/16″ × 5/8″.

Make a saw table setup of dado side cutters with a 1/4″ spacer washer between. Raise the cutters to 3/4″; set the fence to leave a shoulder 5/16″ from the outside surface to the tenon. To do.this, measure from the fence to the nearest side of the spacer washer.

Mark the outside surface of each skirt piece with an X. Up-end a skirt

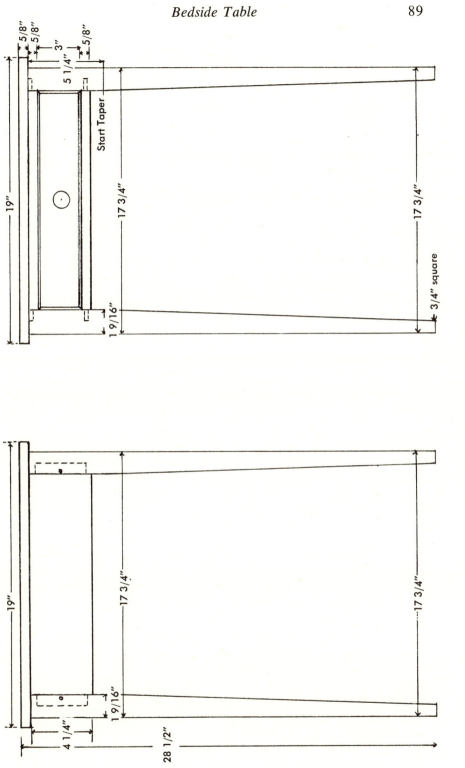

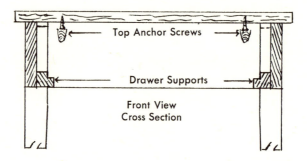

Top Anchor Screws

Drawer Supports

Front View
Cross Section

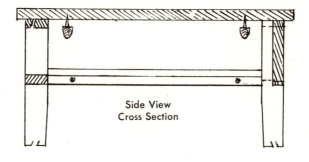

Side View
Cross Section

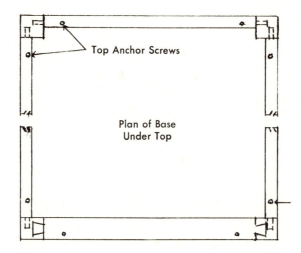

Top Anchor Screws

Plan of Base
Under Top

piece on the table with the X side against the fence. Pass over the dado. Repeat with each end of each skirt piece, including the lower front strip. Hold this piece with the 1 9/16″ surface against the fence. For the upper front strip, the fence must be shifted to cut the 3/4″ tenon completely on one side of the strip. This will leave a 3/8″ shoulder on one side and no shoulder on the other. Check with the "Plan of base under top" on drawing to see that a dovetail is cut on each end. The object of reducing the tail thickness is to lessen the wood removal to seat the tail into the top of leg and still provide a strong cross support.

The two side and one back skirt pieces must have a 3/8″ shoulder cut on the upper and lower edge of each tenon so the mortise will not have to be cut through to the top end of the leg. If it were cut through to the end, the walls of the mortise would be weakened considerably.

Cut a 1/4″ shoulder, front and back, on each end of the lower front strip to leave an approximate one-inch horizontal tenon. Instead of cutting straight sides on the upper strip, angle the cuts to form a tail rather than a tenon.

Mark the upper and lower mortise endings on the chosen leg surfaces

Cross Section
Drawer Front

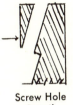

Mortise and
Tenon Detail

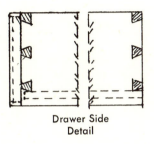

Drawer Side
Detail

Screw Hole
Detail

(for side and back pieces). The lower front strip tenons must be measured accurately so corresponding mortise markings may be made on the legs to place the strip 4 1/4″ from the leg top.

Make a drill press setup for mortises. Clamp a fence 5/16″ in back of the chucked 1/4″ drill. Drill a series of holes (mortise and tenon detail on drawing) between markings on sides and back leg surfaces. Lower front strip mortise must be carefully drilled between parallel lines.

Cut the mortise walls to straight parallel lines using 1/2″ or 3/4″ chisel on long sides and 3/16″ width to square ends. Trial-fit tenons into mortises. Upper front strip is not marked, cut, or fitted at this time.

All inside right-angle surfaces of legs should be sanded before assembly. Start with a side skirt. Select a front and a back leg being sure the mortises for front and back skirts are on the same side. Coat the mortise with glue, also glue the long sides of tenons. Assemble; place in bar clamp, draw tight; be sure top edge of skirt is flush with top of legs. Repeat with second side. Now coat all remaining mortises and tenons (except upper front strip) with glue, insert tenons with hand pressure; span the two bar clamps with two more, lining them up visually with the frame. Place the upper front strip in position with the shoulders turned down between the legs. This is done to keep the front legs parallel when the last two clamps are drawn tight. Check with a large square. If any adjustment is necessary, angle the last two clamps one way or the other to bring the frame into square.

After overnight glue setting, remove clamps, accurately position upper front strip, outline tails with a scribe; chop to a depth of 1/4″, as explained in the chapter on dovetailing. Clean out remaining waste wood to the scribed lines; trial-fit, glue, tap in place, angle and drive in a 1″ head nail in each leg to keep the strip seated firmly until the glue dries. Bore one 3/16″ dowel hole through each mortise and tenon joint. Start the drill about 1/8″ in on the leg surface (side view on drawing), drill about 1″ deep. These pins are inserted in each joint of the sides and back, not the front strips.

All outside surfaces must now be sanded first with coarse paper to eliminate planer marks and any unevenness resulting at joints. Follow with 3/0.

Observe the front view cross section on drawing to understand what must be done to the drawer supports. Start with two pieces about 1 1/4″ × 1 1/4″ × 16″ long. Cut a rabbet into the top corner measured to leave enough wood to be flush with the inside leg surface and 5/8″ thickness to match lower front strip. Bore two screw clearance holes through the full width (lower part) for attachment to side skirt.

Size the drawer front to fit the opening, approximately 1/32″ space all around, and two side pieces of 3/8″ poplar 16″ long by the height of drawer front, one back piece the exact length of the drawer front and 1/2″ less than the height of the sides.

Make a 1/4″ dado setup on the saw table; raise the cutter to 3/16″. Set the fence for a 1/2″ top of groove cut. Pass the inside surface of sides and front over the dado to provide for insertion of the bottom board when drawer is assembled.

To finish work on the drawer, follow the chapter on dovetailing. After assembly, cut a rabbet around the drawer front in the following manner: Mount a thin saw blade on the arbor, raise to cut 3/8″ high. Set the fence to cut 3/32″ in width, place the drawer front surface on the table, press to the fence and pass the front over the saw on all four sides. Make thin stripping 3/32″ × 7/16″, round one 3/32″ edge, miter the two long pieces first, attach to front with thin 1/2″ brads. Cut end pieces to fit and brad in place. Glue up, size, and sand the bottom board; cut a 1/4″ × 1/4″ tongue on the top edge of three sides; insert in bottom groove, drive 2 nails through bottom board into the back piece to hold it in place. Slide the drawer into the opening provided, have it protrude about 1/16″ past the case surface; measure accurately the distance remaining between the case back and the back of drawer. Cut 2 blocks to fill this gap, glue one surface of each and rub onto the back (as you would a rub block) near where each end of the drawer will touch them.

Glue 20″ long random-width boards 5/8″ thick to make up to not less than 19″ wide for the top. After overnight gluing, square to 19″ × 19″. Thoroughly sand top and edge surfaces. Slope screw holes in skirt pieces as shown on drawing for top fastening. Place top upside down, center table base on top, clamp to keep from shifting, seat all screws. Screw holes in the upper front strip are drilled about 3/8″ from the outside edge, sloped slightly to clear the screwdriver.

Countersink these holes and use one-inch #6 flathead screws. To keep the drawer from rocking, fasten a piece of scrap wood 5/8″ thick cut to fit between the upper front strip and the back skirt.

IF THIS TABLE IS MADE OF WALNUT, THE SUGGESTED STAIN MIX IS

    5/8 English oak
    1/4 Danish walnut
    1/8 American cherry

FOR CHERRY

    1/2 Danish walnut
    3/8 English oak
    1/8 American cherry

· 15 ·

Splayed Leg Table
Circa 1760

List of Materials

Rough measurements except leg blanks.

top	17″ wide × 25″ long × 3/4″ thick
legs (4)	1 1/4″ × 1 1/4″ × 27 1/4″ long
skirting (2 sides)	5″ wide × 22″ long × 3/4″ thick
skirting (1 back)	5″ wide × 14″ long × 3/4″ thick
skirting (1 front)	1″ wide × 14″ long × 3/4″ thick
skirting (1 front)	1 3/8″ wide × 14″ long × 3/4″ thick
drawer front	3″ wide × 13″ long × 3/4″ thick

3/8″ thick poplar to make drawer sides, back, and bottom
1″ brushed-brass round knob for drawer pull

Most everyone falls in love with this table because of its intriguing details, popular size, and balanced proportions. We suggest either cherry or walnut. The original from which we make our copies is walnut.

It is common practice to prepare the legs first. After four legs have been sized to 1 1/4″ × 1 1/4″ × 27 1/4″ long, select two right-angle surfaces of each leg to be used for the outside faces. Mark these areas near the leg ends chosen for the tops (if there is a preference).

Legs are sometimes tapered on all four sides but not in this case. Tapering is done only on the two inside surfaces of each leg. This is accomplished easily and neatly on the jointer. Mark the far jointer bed as an indication of where to lay an inside surface of a leg so as to start cutting 6 1/2″ down from the leg top. Continue each cut clear of the bottom end. The number of passes over the jointer on each surface will be determined by the cutting depth setting. Your objective is a final measurement at bottom ends of legs 3/4″ × 3/4″ (see scaled drawing).

Now size all skirting parts—first, the two sides 4 3/4″ × 20 7/8″ long, 90° ends. Cut back and front pieces to widths before length-sizing. As indicated on drawing, back is 4 3/4″, top 1″, bottom front 1 3/8″. To get the desired leg splay, set your crosscut gauge 2° off 90°. Crosscut one end of back skirt; mark the top edge exactly 12 3/4″; crosscut to the mark. The top front piece is to match in length the top edge of the back skirt (crosscut front pieces on the same gauge setting 2°). Crosscut the front bottom piece to the exact measurement of the bottom edge of back skirt. When doing further work on the front bottom, remember that the longer edge is the extreme bottom.

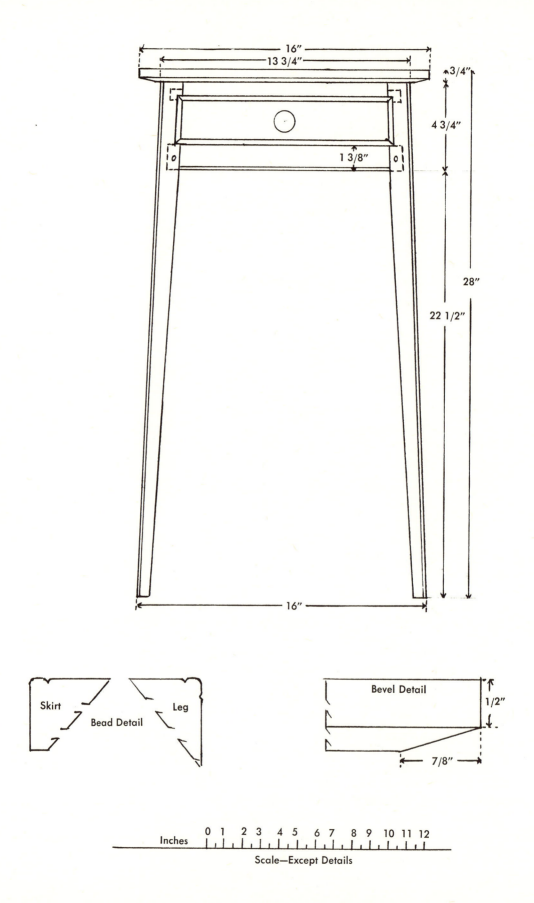

16"

13 3/4"

3/4"

4 3/4"

1 3/8"

28"

22 1/2"

16"

Skirt

Leg

Bead Detail

Bevel Detail

1/2"

7/8"

Inches   0 1 2 3 4 5 6 7 8 9 10 11 12

Scale—Except Details

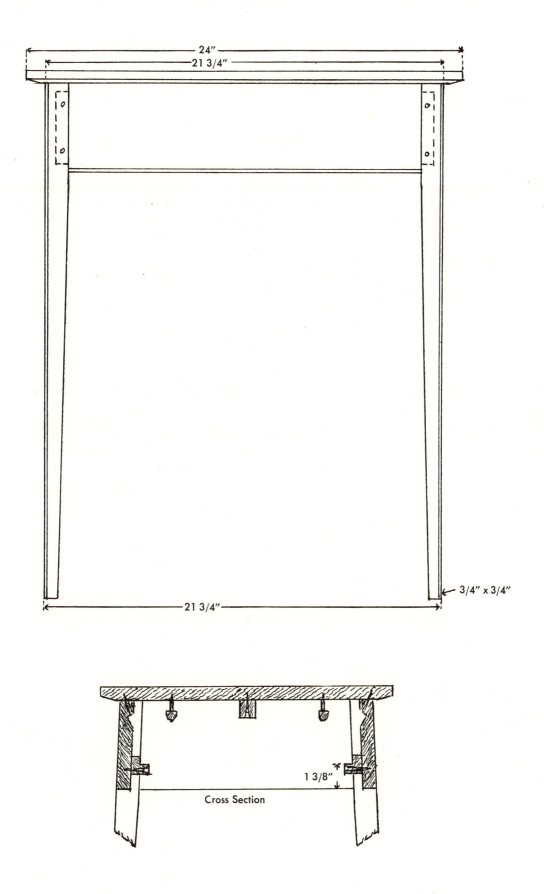

24"

21 3/4"

3/4" x 3/4"

21 3/4"

1 3/8"

Cross Section

Your shop equipment should include a multiple cutter dado head. If this is so, mill the tenons on skirting ends as follows: make a wooden spacer washer exactly 1/4″ thick and place on the saw-table spindle between the two dado side cutters. Make the cutter depth setting 3/4″. Set the ripping fence to leave a 5/16″ outside shoulder (see drawing). Mark all skirt pieces on the chosen outside surface. Pass each skirt piece, end up and marked surface against fence, over the tenoning setup.

Replace cutters with a combination blade, set fence to cut 3/4″ (including saw thickness) and a depth setting of 5/16″. Pass each skirting end, outside surface down, over this saw setting. Reset depth setting 3/16″, pass each end over the saw with the outside surface up. You now have 1/4″ × 3/4″ tenons the full width on all skirt parts.

Because of the 2° angle of front and back skirt ends, it will be more convenient to cut top and bottom shoulders either on a band-saw or by use of a handsaw rather than a double setup on the saw table which is usual with true right-angle ends. Excepting the two front pieces, pencil-mark each tenon 3/8″ down from the top and the same up from the bottom. Band-saw or handsaw to these lines; then cut along and even with tenon shoulders to remove the waste pieces of tenon wood. Leave the tenons full width on the bottom front skirt piece. Cut 3/8″ top edge shoulders similar to side and back skirt pieces on the top front piece; leave bottom edge full.

Mark the legs for mortises in the following manner: group the four legs in a square, top ends up. Check to be sure that all tapered surfaces are inside. Pencil-mark two F's on the leg ends close to the leg surface that

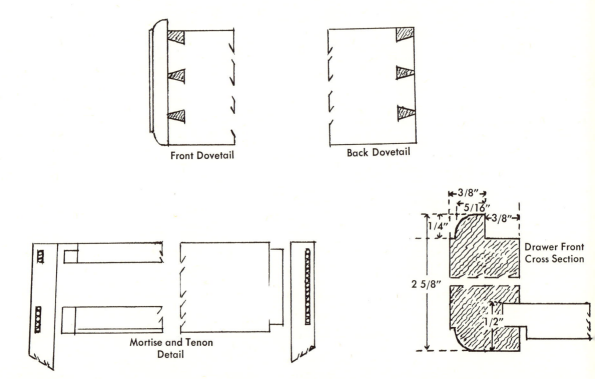

Front Dovetail

Back Dovetail

Mortise and Tenon Detail

Drawer Front Cross Section

will be mortised for the front skirt pieces. Mark four S's in like manner
for the sides and two B's close to the intended back mortise surfaces. When
the legs are separated from their group position, you still know from the
original marks which are the outside surfaces.

Now pencil-mark for mortise endings on each indicated leg surface, that
is, for sides and back, cross lines 3/8″ down from the top end and more
lines 4 3/8″ down to indicate the lower ending of mortises. The leg surfaces
to receive the four front tenons will be marked accordingly, that is, the top
mortise lines 3/8″ and 1″ down. For the bottom piece, mark 3 3/8″ and
4 3/4″ down from leg ends.

Set up your drill press for boring 1/4″ holes 13/16″ deep. Adjust and
clamp a back fence leaving a 5/16″ space between fence and drill. Bore a
line of holes in each mortise area with the marked outside surface held
firmly against the fence (see drawing).

Grip each leg in the vise to chop out the line hole radii with 1/2″ or
3/4″ chisel. Square out mortise ends with a narrow chisel, about 3/16″
wide. Try the tenon in each finished mortise for snug fit.

Next, form the interesting beads on the extreme outer corner of each leg
(the entire length) and on the bottom outside corner (see photo and
drawing) of each side skirt, the back and lower front skirt pieces. This
work can be performed easily by setting a scratch gauge to 3/16″. Scratch
a line the full length on each right-angle surface that forms the outer
corner of each leg. Scratch not once but a number of times to make the
marks reasonably deep. Scratch-line the skirt pieces on the outside surfaces
at the bottom edge only. Use a small block plane to round slightly the
sharp corners; this will result in a rounded bead appearance.

Make a wood sand block about 4″ long, 2″ wide, 1/4″ thick. On one 4″
long edge, plane both sides to form a slender taper, ending in a near
feather edge. Wrap the block with single thickness coarse sand paper, hand
grip the block, press the paper covered tapered edge into the scratched
groove, and sand smooth. In the process of smoothing, try to deepen the
groove also. Repeat with fine paper. Using a paper-covered flat cork block,
sand the rounded corner formed by the plane. Repeat with 3/0 finishing
paper. Sand with coarse and fine paper all tapered inside leg surfaces. Legs
and skirt parts are now ready to assemble with glue.

Coat the leg mortises for one side with glue; coat the tenons on the
matching skirt for that side; seat by hand pressure. Adjust a bar
clamp to span the two legs (use cushion blocks to prevent clamp jaws
marking the legs when pressure is applied). Tighten clamp; inspect joints
for perfect fit. Repeat with the other side parts. Now glue-coat the front
and back mortises of one clamped side assembly; coat *all* the tenons on
front and back skirt pieces. Hand-seat the proper tenons into their intended
mortises in the glue-coated side assembly. Coat mortises in the remaining
side assembly; hand-seat the matching tenons. Stand the table base upright;
using two more bar clamps, span the side clamps at front and back; tighten
these clamps simultaneously; inspect for close-fitting joints; check for

square corners. Should the complete assembly be out of square, loosen both last placed clamps; shift both clamps slightly off parallel with the table line; again tighten and check. If the assembly is further out of square, the clamp shift was made in the wrong direction; adjust for perfect correction. Allow overnight glue setting.

After removing clamps, bore 3/16″ holes through mortise and tenon joints to a depth of one inch, as indicated on drawing; saw to about 1 1/8″ lengths ten pieces from a 3/16″ dowel stick. Glue-coat the holes and drive in the precut pins. Chisel off protruding pin ends.

All outside surfaces may now be sanded. Check with sanding instructions for a complete understanding of procedure necessary for satisfactory results.

Illustrated on the drawing is a cross section showing the drawer runners in correct position. These two pieces may be made of any scrap wood to fit between front and back legs on each side, suggested width and thickness about one inch each way. The surface planned to fit against the side skirt must be angled to 2°. What will be the top inside corner must be cut away leaving a side surface about 1/2″ high that, when positioned, will be flush with the inside surfaces of the front legs. Horizontal or drawer runner surfaces should be cut to leave full width wood on the bottom about 1/2″ thick. The only important measurement when milling these pieces is that the side surface will be flush with legs at the drawer opening. Bore two screw holes in each piece for attachment to skirts with 1 1/4″ #7 screws. Fasten in place as indicated, keeping the drawer runner surfaces even with the bottom drawer opening line.

The cross section also shows angled screw holes for top attachment. These are placed about 2″ in from the ends on back and side skirts. Holes are bored straight through the top front skirt and countersunk.

It is almost certain that a sufficiently wide board cannot be procured for the table top so two or more pieces must be glued edge to edge to make the necessary width. Joint the edge of the pieces you select; adjust two bar clamps, and place on the worktable spreading them so as to put pressure on the top boards near the ends. Position on these clamps the top board pieces as you want them joined. Adjust a top clamp for center pressure. Glue all joining edges; lightly tighten clamps; tap all pieces in place for an even surface; draw tight the three clamps.

After overnight glue-setting, rough-sand both top and bottom surfaces of the tabletop. Saw to 16″ width; square-cut ends for 24″ finished length. As indicated on drawing, the bottom surface is beveled to show only 1/2″ of edge wood. To accomplish this, tilt the circular saw to an angle that will leave a beveled surface 7/8″ wide. Cut the bevel on all four sides holding the tabletop, edge up, when making the four cuts. Coarse- and fine-sand the beveled surfaces. Finish-sand all edges, then attach top to base.

Cut to width the four pieces for the drawer. The front piece will be cut 1/4″ wider than the drawer opening height. This extra width provides for a 1/4″ lip on the top edge. Cut the sides, in width, to match opening height, the back piece, 1/2″ less than opening height.

Square-cut the two side piece ends to 18 1/8". Set crosscut gauge to 2° off 90°. Cut drawer front 1/2" longer than opening (extra length allows for 1/4" lip on each side). Cut back piece to drawer opening width.

Rabbet out what will be the inside right-angle points of the drawer front, sides and top. Set the circular saw to a depth of 3/8" (thickness of side wood). Set the fence for a 1/4" cut, including blade width. Make this cut on both sides and top, placing the inside drawer front surface on saw table. Reset saw blade for a 1/4" depth cut. Reset fence for a 3/8" cut (including saw blade). Make this cut on the three edges holding the drawer front piece edge up with the inside surface against the fence. The front piece should now have a protruding shoulder on the front half thickness that measures 1/4" wide by 3/8" thick. The inside surface should measure, and also fit easily into the drawer opening. You will probably bypass some trouble with the completed drawer binding if this rabbet cut is made to allow about a 1/16" play up and down, also sideways, when placed in the opening for trial fit. When finally cut to finished size, check the back piece to be sure they match in width.

Now the sides and inside surface of the front piece must be grooved for the bottom board. Instructions for this work can be found in the chapter on dovetailing. The only variation is the bottom board thickness which will necessitate the 1/4" groove being milled 1/8" higher up the sides and inside front. Also the 3/8" thick bottom board must have a clearance shoulder cut on the lower surface leaving a 1/4" tongue to slide into the receiving grooves.

When dovetailing is completed, work the thumbnail molding around the front surface (see drawing), in the following manner: Set the circular saw blade to cut to a depth of 1/4". Set the ripping fence to cut 1/16" less than the front piece thickness. Edge up the front piece holding the back surface against the fence; saw all four edges. Quarter-round the remaining right-angle shoulders with a block plane. Finish-sand all drawer parts.

Assemble the drawer with glue, coating only the tails; position and tap to seat firmly the side pieces; slide the drawer into its opening even if it is a tight fit; allow overnight glue setting. Remove and determine what surface may be binding, if any. Work down that particular area with a plane or coarse sandpaper to a smooth, nonbinding fit. Glue up, cut to size, shoulder, and sand the bottom board. Two or three holding nails through the bottom panel into the 3/8" edge of back piece completes the drawer—and table.

IF IT IS MADE OF WALNUT USE THE FOLLOWING STAIN MIX

> 5/8 English oak
> 1/4 Danish walnut
> 1/8 American cherry

FOR CHERRY

> 1/2 Danish walnut
> 3/8 English oak
> 1/8 American cherry

·16·

Low Post Bed Frame

List of Materials

All measurements are finished sizes.

head posts	(2)	2 3/8″ × 2 3/8″ × 36 5/8″ long
foot posts	(2)	2 3/8″ × 2 3/8″ × 27 1/8″ long
end rails	(2)	4″ wide × 1 5/8″ thick × 40 1/2″ long
side rails	(2)	4″ wide × 1 5/8″ thick × 77 1/2″ long
head board		17″ wide × 3/4″ thick × 41″ long
slats	(2)	3″ wide × 3/4″ thick × 39 3/4″ long
slat supports	(2)	1″ × 3/4″ × 76″ long
bolts with		
square nuts	(4)	3/8″ × 6″
bed bolt covers	(2)	
glides	(4)	1 1/2″ "No Mar" socket type

This bed is sized, between rails, to accommodate a standard twin-size spring and mattress, 3 feet 3 inches by 6 feet long. There are now, in addition to the standard double-size, a queen, king, and probably others. If a size other than the twin illustrated is desired, procure and measure the spring and mattress before making the frame. The only changes to be made are the extra inches to be added to the four rails, head board, and length of slats. The bed photographed is made of cherry. It would also look good if made of pine, walnut, or maple.

If the bed is made of pine, then pine is used throughout. When other woods are used, the head rail and side rails are made of poplar because this wood is less expensive and when the bed is made up the side rails are always covered.

Try to find 2 1/2″ thick wood for posts; if not available, 3″ must be used. Mill to 2 3/8″ × 2 3/8″ × 37 1/8″ long for the head posts; this is 1/2″ added for lathe center cutoff on the top end after turning. The length of foot posts is 27 1/8″ plus 1/2″ for cutoff. Carefully mark for the lathe centers; mount a blank in the lathe and try for balance; if there is too much vibration, reduce the rpm until enough wood has been turned off to bring it more in balance. This procedure may be necessary when turning a piece of this thickness. Check with the drawing to locate and pencil-mark positions for the portion which will remain square.

Trying to teach woodturning is almost useless; cause and effect are the main ingredients and causes are too difficult to explain. The old saw fits the situation ideally, "Experience is the best teacher." A few don'ts are in order: Don't use a piece of wood that has a severe flaw in it; the wood will be weakened at that point and will possibly break under pressure of the turning tool. Don't use excessive speed; slow rpm to control vibration. Don't use dull tools.

After turning the posts, remove the 1/2″ of waste wood from the post tops, sanding to a finished smoothness. Before mortising for rails and head board, it is best to have the tenons cut and measured. Glue 3/4″ boards to make a head board 17″ wide by a rough length of 42″. Mill all four rails to width and thickness first, then to finished length: end rails 40 1/2″, side rails 77 1/2″. A 3/4″ tenon on all rail ends should be centered side to side and top to bottom which means a shoulder is cut on each side of each rail end 3/4″ from the end and 7/16″ in toward the center thickness. Use the same saw setup to shoulder tops and bottoms. Raise the saw blade to 3/4″; make a fence setting to cut away 7/16″; up-end a rail; pass over saw holding the rail against the fence; cut sides, top, and bottom; this should leave a tenon 3/4″ long, 3/4″ wide and 3 1/8″ high; repeat.

Cut the mortises at this time. Chuck a 3/4″ bit in the drill press; set the fence to bit center exactly one half of 2 3/8″; set the bit stop to bottom at exactly 13/16″. Mark two right-angle sides of each post 3 1/4″ in the center of the 9″ square from top to bottom; drill a series of holes in line, sinking the top and bottom holes first, then two in the center; complete drilling on all four posts.

According to the mortises pair the head and foot posts for right and left—be sure to mark the proper surfaces for bolt holes (cross section post and rail). Do bolt hole-boring and counterboring before moving the drill press fence setting. Counterbore first; mark the surface opposite the side rail mortise at a point that will be the mortise center vertically; chuck a 1 1/8″ bit; hold the post firmly against the fence and counterbore about 1/16″ deeper than the bolt head plus a washer. Repeat on the three other posts. Replace the 1 1/8″ bit with a 7/16″; more this hole all the way through in the center of the counterbore.

Now all eight mortises must be squared out with hand tools. When working on those for head and foot rails, carefully cut them for a tight fit because the rails will be glued in permanently; side rail mortises should allow the rails to slip in and out easily. The rail ends may not be interchangeable so when boring for bolts, mark in the close area on the inside rail and post an X with the 1/2″ chisel, the next end with X X and so forth. Stand posts in their proper corners—as though looking at the bed from the foot end; have a side rail gripped in the vise vertically with the top

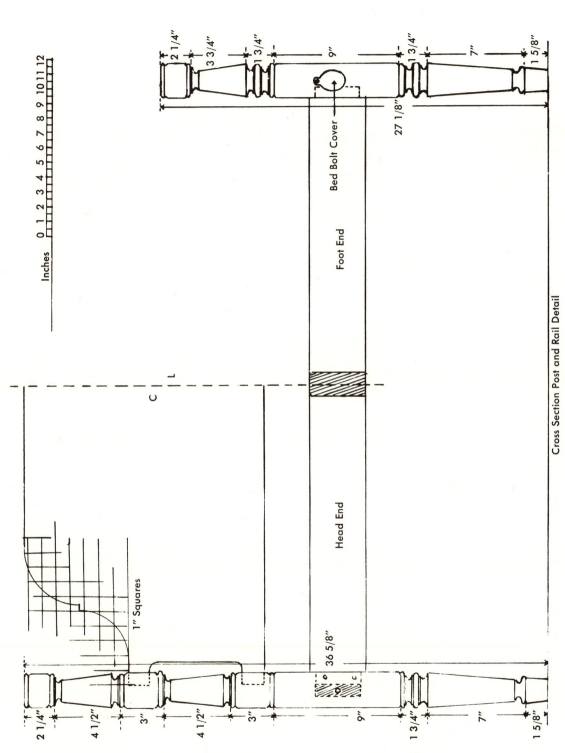

Inches 0 1 2 3 4 5 6 7 8 9 10 11 12

2 1/4" 3 3/4" 1 3/4" 9" 1 3/4" 7" 1 5/8"

Bed Bolt Cover

Foot End

27 1/8"

Head End

36 5/8"

1" Squares

2 1/4" 4 1/2" 3" 4 1/2" 3" 9" 1 3/4" 7" 1 5/8"

Cross Section Post and Rail Detail

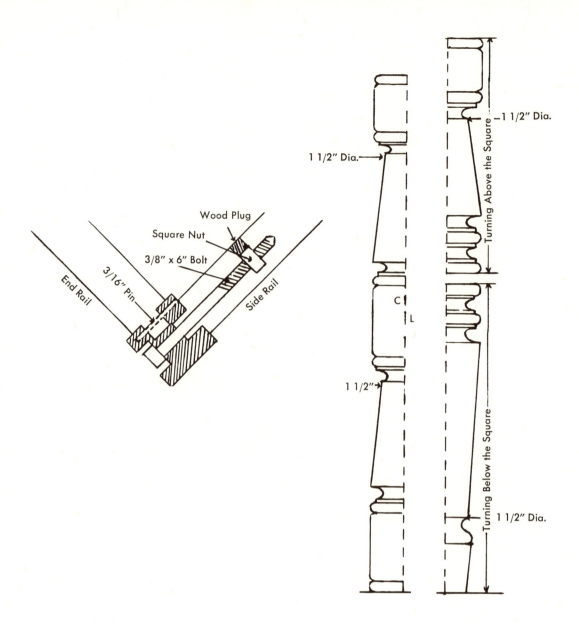

surface up—if there is a choice, the inside to the left looking at it from the foot end; insert the tenon into the right foot post mortise. Using a 7/16″ bit in the brace, pass the bit through the post hole and give the brace a few turns to mark the rail end for complete boring; identify rail and post with X mark. Turn rail end for end (the inside is now on the right and the head end is toward you); place the right head post on tenon; mark with brace and bit; mark with X X. Use the same procedure on the left side.

Work on the head board next. Square it for finished length; mark for two tenons on each end (check with drawing). The lower tenon starts at the board bottom and is 1 1/2″ high; the upper one starts at 8″ up and ends at 9 1/2″. Center a 3/4″ bit one inch in from the end to form the radius between tenons (check with drawing); bore through board thickness; do the other radii the same way; band-saw the straight line between radii. Above the upper tenon, mark the board with one-inch squares, as shown on the drawing; either freehand or with a compass, follow the line as shown; band-saw; repeat other end. Finish-sand all edges. Rough-sand front and back surfaces; finish-sand front surface.

The head posts have been turned so as to place the head board starting point 3″ above the top of rail; mark for lower mortise at this point. Measure tenons and mark for corresponding mortises on posts. Use either drill press or brace and bit to make these 3/4″ wide × 1″ deep × 1 1/2″ long mortises. Square-out with hand tools.

Rough-and finish-sand all unturned post surfaces. The head rail should have only the sharp corners sanded. The foot rail must have the top corners well rounded; sand the sharpness off the bottom corners. Rough-and finish-sand top and outside surfaces.

Head and foot assemblies may now be made. Coat the head rail mortises with glue; coat the rail tenons with glue; lay one post (mortise side up) on worktable; insert rail tenon into mortise; insert head board into mortises without glue—be sure to have the face surface to the front. Fit the other post (mortise side down) in place; lay the assembly on a bar clamp lined up with the rail and tighten. Assemble the foot end in the same way. After overnight setting, bore 2 holes for 3/16″ dowel pins in each post and tenon as shown on drawing. Coat holes with glue and drive in pins; chisel off excess pin wood and sand.

Again, grip in the vise each rail positioned as before for bolt hole boring. If your equipment includes a 7/16″ twist drill which can be used with an electric portable drill, boring bolt holes will be considerably easier; if not, a brace and bit must be used. Insert a bolt with washer under the head, through the bolt hole in a post; measure the length of bolt protruding from the post surface; this distance plus 1/2″ for safety, will be how deep the hole must be bored from the rail shoulder. Bore each hole to the full depth, checking often to keep in line both horizontally and vertically.

After boring, grip one end of a rail in the vise with the inside surface up; insert a length of 3/8″ dowel rod to show direction of hole; draw a pencil line over what appears to be the center of hole in width. About 3/4″ from the end of the bolt when seated, mark a right-angle line for a nut slot. This slot will be about 1″ long by probably 7/16″ wide and in depth, should come to within 1/4″ of the under or face side. Square out this slot with a small chisel. Grind a stubby point on each bolt for less difficulty in starting into the embedded nut. Clean out all wood chips from both the slot and bolt hole; drop a nut into the slot; see that it is down to the bottom of slot; insert a bolt with washer in hole and engage the nut thread. Draw the bolt up tight to hold the nut in position; have a strip of plug wood ready; chisel off the four corners and drive into slot until it seats on the nut. Seating will be apparent if one hand is held on the bolt when driving in the plug;

use a heavy hammer on the bolt head to free it for easy turning. Lay a back saw flat on rail surface to cut off plug wood; hand-plane plug for a smooth surface. Repeat with 3 more rail ends. Well-round the top corners of rails; smooth bottom corners; rough- and fine-sand top and outside surfaces.

To support the slats, make two strips 1" wide × 3/4" thick × 75" long; at about 12" from each end, notch out for slats—the notches should be about 3 1/4" wide by 1/4" deep (from top down). Bore for 1 1/4" screws—one hole near the end, another about 2" from notch, one under notch, and another 2" past the notch. Bring all strip ends up to this point; position strips flush with bottom of rails; sink screws. Length of slats should be 39 3/4".

Conforming to the basic pattern of this book which is "to be able to procure all materials locally," it will be noted that a cover of some kind is needed for the two bolts through the foot posts. Since no brass ones are available locally, we have made a pair of contrasting wood 1/8" thick; these may not be as desirable as brass but look surprisingly well at that.

THE STAIN MIX FOR CHERRY IS

7/8 Danish walnut
1/8 American cherry

·17·

Chest of Drawers

LIST OF MATERIALS

Lumber will be given here in square feet of each thickness.
12 ft. × 3/4" thick
4 ft. × 3/4" poplar for frame interior
12 ft. × 5/8" thick
30 ft. × 3/8" poplar for drawer sides, backs, and bottoms
back panel 1/4" plywood 24" × 30"
broad brass-plated butt hinges (1 pair) 1 1/2" × 2"
"Amerock" 3" drawer pulls (5)
brass knobs (2) 5/8" diameter

This chest was chosen for its many potential uses: in the living room or reception hall as a wall piece with a lamp; again in the living room with the leaf turned over for that hurryup note that must be written. In the bedroom, it can also serve as a dressing table. Size is not restricted except for height if the writing leaf is to be used occasionally.

The chest photographed is made of cherry but the design is simple enough to use pine or maple, if desired. Should pine be chosen, all lumber in the list of materials would be pine instead of some poplar.

Cut enough 3/4″ thick board lengths 26″ long to glue up two side panels each 15″ wide; square to 25 1/8″ × 15″ when removed from the clamps. Rough-sand both side surfaces of each panel. It can be readily observed on the plan at frame under top that a 1/2″ × 1 inch strip has been added on the front inside edge of each panel to provide the necessary extra thickness in the chamfered corner area. These pieces are sized to the exact length of the side panels and are to be grooved for division frames when setups are made for side panel milling.

Mount the 3/4″ wide dado on the saw arbor; set height for 1/8″; set fence for first groove to cut 3/4″ wide from panel end. Check cut with a piece of wood to be used for division frames—when placed in the groove, frame wood should be flush with the panel end. Choose and mark the front edge of each side panel. When milling the division frame grooves, stop the dado cut just short of the front corner. For half of the number of grooves it will be necessary to lower the panel down on the saw table at a premarked spot so the groove does not cut through the front corner. Groove each end of each panel and each end of what we will call filler strips. These grooves on filler strips are to be cut on the one-inch surface, not the 1/2″ edge.

Milling from the top down, set fence 3 3/4″ to the near side of cutter—which means the 3/4″ groove starts at 3 3/4″ from panel end and ends in width at 4 1/2″. Pass top of panels and top of strips over dado—to groove narrow strips, use crosscut gauge in conjunction with fence. Now groove for the next frame. Exactly 8″ to the near side—pass all units over dado. Next groove 12 3/4″ to the near side. Reverse panel units to cut from bottom end upward for the last division cut. Set fence to cut exactly 6″ to the near side.

Rabbet out the inside (grooved side) back corners for the 1/4″ ply-wood panel—from front to back about 5/16″, from inside toward outside 3/8″. Bore five 5/32″ screw holes through each filler strip, more or less equal distance apart; countersink on grooved side. Have 3/4″ #6 screws ready for strip attachment. Coat the smooth side (not grooved) of a strip with glue, position it exactly flush with the front edge of a side panel and exactly in place from top to bottom; make sure grooves match grooves in side panel; seat all five screws. Repeat.

As shown on the plan, the front corners must be chamfered. Tilt the saw

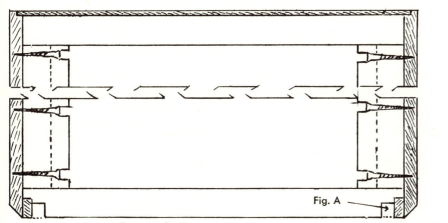

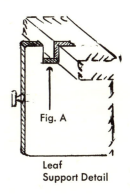

Leaf
Support Detail

Fig. A

Plan at Frame Under Top

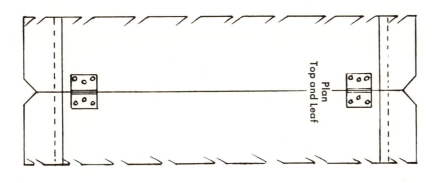

Plan
Top and Leaf

arbor to 45°; set fence so as to cut 3/4″ from the corner of each right-angle surface. Remove saw marks with hand plane.

Six division frames are to be made next. Observe the plan of frame top. The two upper frames serve a double purpose, supporting the drawer and the support slide for writing leaf. The side members for these two frames must be of sufficient width to provide for first 1/8″ groove inside, 1/2″ filler strip, 3/4″ slide, 3/4″ facing strip between slide and drawer plus 3/8″ for drawer slide to ride on. All added together, side members must be 2 1/2″ wide. The remaining 4 frames have side members the same width as all front and back pieces, 1 1/2″, as shown by dotted line. The wide side members, as shown on drawing, must be counterbored 1/2″ so 2 1/2″ #8 screws can be used for frame attachment to side panels. The lesser width side members should be bored with an 11/64″ drill for 2″ #8 screws.

Now rip and size all parts for the six frames: front and back pieces 20 3/4″ × 1 1/2″ × 3/4″; wide side pieces (4) 2 1/2″ × 3/4″ × 12 3/4″. This figure is determined by the total depth of frame 14 3/4″ less 1 1/2″ front and 1 1/2″ back plus two 1/2″ tongues. Narrow side pieces 1 1/2″ × 12 3/4″ × 3/4″. Make a dado setup for tongues first— a 1/4″ spacer between the two side cutters; pencil-mark one side of all side members; set fence to leave the 1/4″ tongue at about center of the 3/4″ thick side pieces; raise cutters to 1/2″ plus in height. Pass both ends of all side pieces over this setup; keep marked side against fence.

Before changing back to saw blade, remove spacer from saw arbor, using only the two side cutters for a 1/4″ groove; raise the cutters slightly above the previous setting. Mark one side of each front and back piece; hold marked side against fence; cut in (full depth) to about 4″. The end toward you must be lowered onto the saw table. Repeat all pieces. Change to saw blade; set fence to cut to a 1/2″ shoulder from the end; position blade in height to remove only the waste wood from each side of tongue. Repeat.

Place two bar clamps on worktable; coat with glue the grooves in one front and one back piece; coat the tongues of two side pieces (in the case of the wide side piece frames, be sure the counterbored holes face to the inside of frame). Fit this frame together; place in clamps and draw up tight; try square; in case of needed adjustment, angle the clamps slightly one way or the other. Ten minutes time in clamps is sufficient; remove carefully. Repeat. After setting, sand flush all flat surface joints and the end joinings where squeezed out glue has hardened.

Now to make these frames fit in place, it will be necessary to cut out all front corners. The cutouts are to be exactly the same dimension as the filler strips, i.e., 1/2″ × 1″. *Do not cut the inch measurement on the front edge.* Mount again the 3/4″ dado setup used for division frames, 3/4″ wide × 1/8″ deep. To set the fence it will be necessary to add a few fractions— 1/8″ into the side panel, 1/2″ thickness of filler strip, and 3/4″ wood thickness of leaf support slide (Fig. A). So the fence must be set 1 3/8″ from the start of 3/4″ groove—these grooves, on the under side of top frame and upper side of second frame; position accurately the vertical dividing piece between support slide and the drawer. Mill these grooves entirely through from front to back. From the top frame only, remove a 3/4″ cube of wood at each end (Fig. A on plan); this allows the raised height block of slide to recess in line with drawer fronts when closed.

Place a side panel on the worktable, grooved side up; arrange all frames for their chosen position; attach each one in its slot with three screws but no glue. Turn the partial assembly over and line it up on the other side panel; carefully seat each frame in its slot before screw fastening. Try square as a complete unit. Cut two vertical dividing pieces to fit into

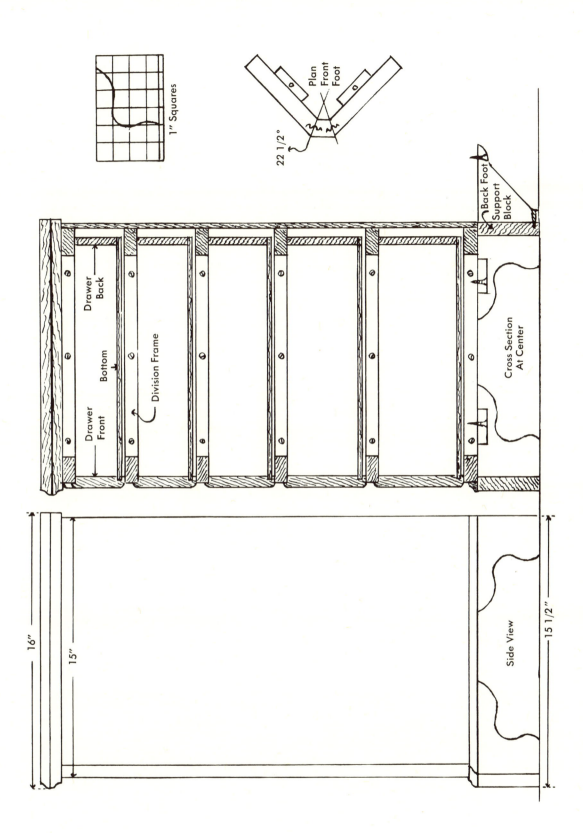

1" Squares

Plan
Front
Foot

22 1/2°

Back Foot

Support Block

Drawer Back

Bottom

Division Frame

Drawer Front

Cross Section At Center

16"

15"

Side View

15 1/2"

grooves provided. These pieces should be about 3 1/4″ in length, 3/4″ thick and about 1 1/2″ wide; width is unimportant. Glue grooves in the area to be filled by the strip; tap in flush with frame fronts. Repeat other side. To keep the drawer and support slide divided and in line, glue a piece fitted to the groove about 1 1/2″ high and the remaining distance from front to back; do both sides, of course. After glue setting, the entire front surface should be rough sanded to a point where no joining member is raised above its neighbor. This will complete all surfaces to the rough-sanded stage; sand all surfaces with #120 (3/0) grit.

Make and apply base molding next; the curves can be whatever your equipment will permit. Keep it to these sizes, 5/8″ high × 1/2″ thick (front to back). Miter to 22 1/2° the front piece first; brad in place using 1″ #18 brads. Miter right and left side pieces; brad in place—carefully fit a piece for each chamfer and brad.

Before starting the feet, make a pattern by following the one-inch scaled blocks on drawing. Use any available stiff material, preferably thin. As the blocks indicate, the pattern should be 3 3/4″ high and 5 1/4″ wide.

Saw a piece of 3/4″ wood 3 3/4″ by about 40″ long; this length will allow extra wood for more accuracy when mitering at right angle. Cut from this length a piece 11″ long with squared 90° ends for the two back feet. Place the top edge of pattern on an 11″ edge of wood; mark the curve; turn pattern end for end (not upside down); place on the lower 11″ edge; mark. Now tilt the saw blade to 22 1/2°; use crosscut gauge for a true right-angle cut; saw one end of the foot wood; measure 10″ from the longest angle surface which will be the face side; when making the second 10″ cut, keep the face side 10″—that will make the underside only about 9 1/4″ long. This is important because placing the pattern for marking as was done with the back feet and turning it end for end results in two half feet either right or left, depending on which side of the pattern is up. Cut another 10″ piece exactly like the first one; when marking this piece, turn the pattern *upside down* and repeat marking procedure; you will then have two half feet of the opposite side. All foot parts may now be band-sawn and sawed edges sanded.

The remaining foot wood now has one end squared off on a 22 1/2° angle; measure on the longest side the exact distance of the bottom edge of base molding on the chamfer line. This will be the wedge piece (plan front foot) to match the complete foot line to the base molding; cut another wedge like it. Probably the closest corrugated fastener obtainable will be 3/8″ × 5—that means 5 corrugations which is two too many. Use nail cutters to break off one corrugation on each side (check with plan front foot). Do the assembling of these feet on a solid surface such as the saw tabletop. Coat the angled edge of one side with glue and one edge of a wedge piece; place the long top edge of foot side on table; match glued edge of wedge; center corrugated fastener on joint and seat with a heavy hammer; turn upside down; seat fastener in the top edge. Repeat with the other wing. Repeat with the other front foot. Cut 6 foot anchor blocks 1/2″ × 1/2″ × 2″ long (shown on cross section at center); glue one on each inside foot wing, keeping blocks flush with the top edges of feet. After glue setting, drill one 5/32″ screw hole down from the top through each block; this is the size for one-inch #7 screws.

As of now, the back feet consist of only one foot side each. Make two back foot support blocks as shown on drawing. Drill 5/32″ screw holes as shown. Rough- and finish-sand all feet. The front feet should follow the molding edge around the corner; hold feet in position to this line; sink tight two anchor screws in each foot. Hold the right-angle squared edge of a back foot even with the end of molding and the outside face of foot piece flush with bottom edge of molding; seat one 1″ #7 screw through the anchor block. Now place the right-angle squared edge of a back support block against the inside end of foot piece; the support should be resting on the surface of bottom frame which is on a line with the molding and foot side piece. Hold support and side pieces together and sink a #7 screw through the support and into the foot side; this keeps the foot side in its proper right-angle position; a screw through the support and into the frame makes the foot strong and rigid. Repeat with other foot.

Saw two leaf support slides 3/4″ × 3″ × 14 1/2″ long. Try-fit these pieces into their openings; hand-plane wherever they seem to be tight; a good sliding fit is desirable. Now blocks to fill the cubed cutouts must be glued to the top edges of slides having the wood grain running from front to back as with the slide itself. The cutout is 3/4″ each way but the block to fill it will be 5/16″ longer from front to back; this provides a wood protrusion to match the lips that will be on drawer fronts. When these blocks become part of the slides, there will not be a need for stop blocks in back because the slides will stop when the height blocks seat themselves in the cutouts.

Saw to size all necessary wood for drawer fronts, sides, and backs. Bottoms can be done later. Accurately measure each drawer opening; saw each front piece 1/4″ larger from bottom to top and 1/2″ longer from side to side. All drawer fronts are made of 5/8″ thick wood. Rabbet out the back edges of sides and tops to leave 1/4″ × 1/4″ lips on the front surfaces. That means a rabbet is 1/4″ wide × 3/8″ from back toward the front. Try to provide at least 1/16″ play when try-fitting the front in its opening. Except for the lips, these drawers are made by following the standard procedure. Sides, backs, and bottoms are of 3/8″ poplar.

Make the double top next, 5/8″ wood must be glued up to provide two panels sized to 16″ wide by 20″ long. The 20″ includes a 1/4″ tongue 1/2″ long on each end. Four battens also will be needed—make these 2 1/4″ wide by 17″ rough length. After rough-sanding the panels to provide a fairly smooth straight surface for milling the tongues, set up the two side dado cutters with a 1/4″ spacer between; raise the cutters to a height of 1/2″; set the fence to place the tongue as near as possible to the center of the 5/8″ thick panel. Pencil-mark one side of panels and also one side of battens. Hold marked side of a panel, up-ended, against the fence; pass over the dado to mill the tongue; repeat two ends of two panels; remove spacer and use 2 side cutters only; raise slightly above previous setting;

adjust fence to place groove exactly in line with the tongue. Hold marked side of batten against fence; pass over dado; repeat with three battens.

Coat tongues of one panel with glue; coat grooves of two battens with glue; hand-seat battens, keeping marked sides facing one way; be sure to have extra wood protruding on each end; place in two bar clamps for tight seating. Repeat with other panel. After setting, continue the panel edge line over the batten ends (both panel side edges); band-saw. For a fully accurate straight line make a light jointer cut the full length of each long edge. Repeat. Rough-sand both sides of each panel.

Open one of the 1 1/2″ butt hinges; lay it flat; measure up to the center of pin, or what would be better is to have a router bit adjusted to the center point of hinge pin. Line up a hinge pin paralleling the edge of top (plan top and leaf) 3″ in from the end; mark with a scriber; rout out close to the line; finish cutting to the line with hand chisels. Bring the other hinge work up to this point. The number screw to use for the hinges will depend upon size of holes; whatever number, the length should be 1/2″. Drill small pilot holes for these screws. Fasten the hinges on the top; butt the leaf up to the top, keeping ends even; press down on hinges and mark with a scriber; rout out; trim to line with chisels; pilot holes; seat screws; fold leaf over on top; see if any edge should be trimmed to meet its counterpart. Before separating the two panels mark and saw the two front corners (plan top and leaf). Along each right-angle edge, make a mark at the 3/4″ point, pencil a straight line from mark to mark; band-saw; repeat.

Remove hinges; run a molding on the two sides and front but not the back edge of each panel; be sure that the molding is cut on the top surface of leaf when closed and the under surface of top; it is suggested that the same molding be used as was cut on base strips. Sand molding. Both sides of leaf and top of top panel can be sanded with an intermediate (80 grit) paper to make removing cross scratches on battens a little easier. After sanding the entire panel, remove cross scratches by sanding with the grain of the battens; do this also with #120 grit. The leaf may be attached with hinges for finishing if so desired.

Bore for top attachment screws next, two screw holes near the ends on front and back edges of top frame, sloping them so the screwdriver will have clearance, one hole through each frame end, about center, sloped and positioned far enough in to give driver clearance. Countersink all holes.

Place top upside down on work table; place case (upside down) on top panel; there should be about 3/4″ overhang on sides and front with 1/4″ protruding in back; sink screws. Fit 1/4″ plywood back; nail in with 1″ #18 head nails. Hardware will be mounted as shown on drawing when finishing is completed.

IF THE CHEST IS OF CHERRY, USE THE CHERRY MIX

7/8 Danish walnut
1/8 American cherry

·18·

Desk on Frame

List of Materials

*Leg wood is given in actual measurements; otherwise ap-
proximate square footage is listed for different thicknesses.*

legs (4)   1 5/8″ × 1 5/8″ × 25″

30 sq. ft. of 3/4″ thick

15 sq. ft. of 3/8″ thick

5 sq. ft. of 5/16″ thick

21 sq. ft, of 1/4″ thick

"Amerock" 1 1/8″ brass-finished knobs (4) only

5/8″ brass-plated knobs (6)

old-fashioned drawer lock or

(second choice) cylinder drawer lock

This is the most important piece illustrated when considering the interest shown by the ladies of the family. It is ideal for the living room or positively a dream for the teenage daughter. The desk illustrated is made of pine but any other cabinet wood would look good.

Mark centers on the 25″ leg blanks; mount a blank in the lathe; mark for the unturned portions, 6 1/4″ down from the top and a line 2″ plus another 5 1/2″ up from the bottom. Turn down to a complete round the indicated sections; using a small gouge and a skew, shape the leg as illustrated. Repeat with the others.

Skirt pieces, front strips above and below drawer opening, and stretchers are all placed to come flush with the outside surfaces of the leg squares. Mill the front strips exactly 1 5/8″ × 3/4″ × 30 1/4″; when the 3/4″ dovetail is cut on each end, the distance between legs will be 28 3/4″. The back skirt is to be the same length 30 1/4″ × 5 1/4″ × 3/4″, two long stretchers 30 1/4″ × 2″ × 3/4″ for front and back, two side skirts 16 7/8″ × 5 1/4″ × 3/4″ thick, two side stretchers 16 7/8″ × 2″ × 3/4″.

Set up the two dado side cutters with a 5/16″ spacer between; fence setting to leave a shoulder 5/16″ from outside surface to tenon; raise the cutters to 3/4″ plus; pencil-mark one side of all pieces; up-end a piece, holding marked side against fence, and pass over dado. Repeat all ends except the front strips. Reset the fence to place the full 5/16″ tenon on the top surface of the strips. Remount the saw blade with a fence setting of 3/4″ to the outside of blade and just high enough to cut through the waste wood forming the front shoulder; remove waste wood; reset height to cut back shoulders; reset height again to cut waste wood from under side of front strips; before changing the fence setting, raise saw blade to 3/8″ height; use crosscut gauge in conjunction with the fence; edge up all pieces (except top and bottom front strips) to make the first cut of 3/8″ × 3/4″ shoulders top and bottom; make these cuts; reset height to 1/4″ and make first shoulder cut on front strips. Reset the fence to cut 3/8″ to the outside of blade; raise to 3/4″ high; still using crosscut gauge, up-end all pieces (except front strips) to finish shoulder cuts; reset fence to 1/4″ outside of blade; finish shoulder cuts on front strips.

So no mistake is made when mortising, stand all four legs upright, grouped in a square. Mark the tops where each mortise is to be cut; leave the front strip leg sides blank. Pencil-mark for length of mortises, 3/8″ and 4 7/8″ down from the top of legs. Now mark for stretcher mortises; up from leg end, mark 3 1/8″ and 4 3/8″; include front stretcher marks.

Chuck a 5/16″ bit or drill in the press; set depth of hole into the legs to 13/16″; set the fence to leave 5/16″ of wood from leg corner to start of mortise. When boring for each mortise, be sure to have the proper leg corner against the fence. Also when boring for a skirt mortise, do the stretcher for that side at the same time. Do not forget to mortise for the front stretcher. Measure and mark for the bottom front strip; this strip will have the tenon placed on the bottom side for convenience in accurate measuring; this mortise will be made at right angle to the leg front surface. Using a square, make two lines across the leg surface, one at 4 15/16″ and the other 5 1/4″ down from the top. Now make a stop mark 1/4″ in from the front corner and another 1/4″ from the back corner. Bore these mortise holes to the same 13/16″ depth. Repeat. Square out all mortises with the appropriate width chisels.

Finish-sand all inside leg squares (mortise surfaces). Rough-sand all skirt outside surfaces. Round the top edge of each stretcher piece (cross section stretcher) and finish-sand top and inside surfaces. All frame parts are ready for assembly.

Select the front and back legs for the right side; coat with glue all mortises for this assembly; coat tenons on right skirt and stretcher; assemble by hand; place in bar clamps one clamp in line with the skirt and the other parallel with the stretcher; tighten both clamps. Repeat with the left side. After at least overnight setting, remove the clamps; coat all remaining mortises and tenons, including the lower front strip; assemble by hand. Before placing the front in bar clamps, temporarily place the top front strip shoulders between the legs to keep the whole front properly aligned; place in clamps; tighten. Repeat with back clamps; try square and adjust if necessary. After setting, bore two 3/16″ holes through each skirt mortise and tenon to a depth of 1 1/4″; also bore one hole into each stretcher joint (see drawing); coat with glue and seat 3/16″ dowel pins. Band-saw ends of top strip to dovetail shape; mark outline with scriber and chop into leg wood to seat strip flush with the top. Chisel off excess pin wood; rough-sand flush, then finish-sand all flat outside surfaces.

Using any scrap wood, make 2 drawer support pieces—check with cross section drawer support—these pieces fit between front and back legs and are fastened to the side skirts. Start with wood about 1 1/2″ × 1 1/2″; rabbet out the top inside corner leaving wood the thickness of the space to be filled from inside surface of skirt to the drawer opening surface of the leg, which is about 7/8″. The right angle cut on the bottom for the drawer to slide on should leave 3/4″ below the cut which makes it convenient when fastening to side. As indicated on drawing, bore 2 holes in each piece for 1 1/4″ #7 screws; countersink; attach to side pieces, holding flush with the skirt bottom edge. Make all drawers after openings are ready for measurement.

Start the desk by gluing together boards to get the necessary widths, side panels finished size 18″ wide by 14 1/2″ long or high, top board 9 1/2″ wide by 30 1/4″ long, writing bed 17 3/4″ wide by 29 1/2″ long. All these panels are 3/4″ thick.

Until all milling is completed on the side panels, keep them in the rectangle form. Rough-sand them inside and out for more accurate milling. Set up the 3/4″ dado to groove for a bottom frame, 3/4″ from bottom edge and 1/8″ deep; shift the fence to cut the writing bed grooves to start 3 3/4″

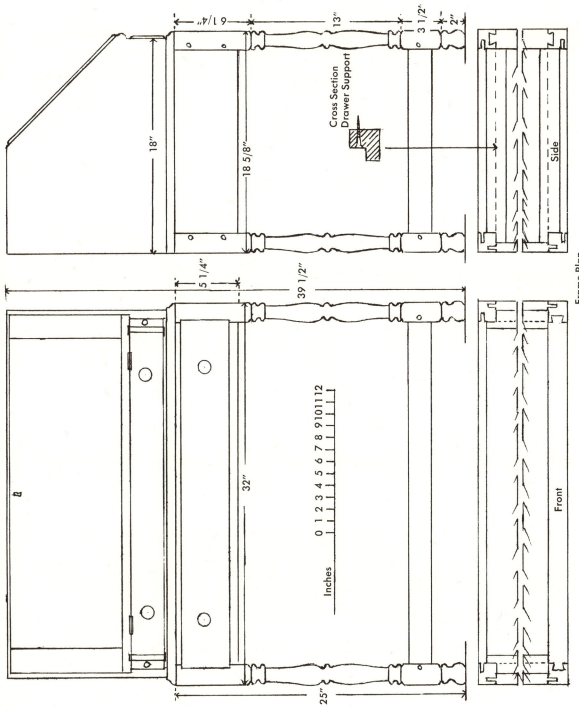

Cross Section
Stretcher

2"

3/4"

6 1/4"

13"

3 1/2"

2"

18"

18 5/8"

Cross Section
Drawer Support

Side

5 1/4"

39 1/2"

32"

0 1 2 3 4 5 6 7 8 9 10 11 12

Inches

Front

25"

Frame Plan

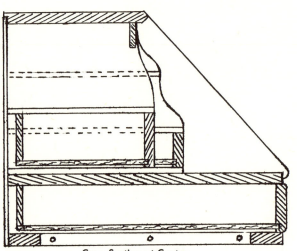

Cross Section at Center

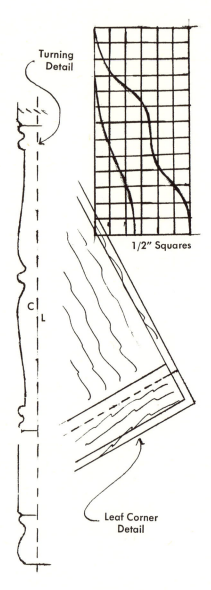

Turning Detail

1/2" Squares

Leaf Corner Detail

C L

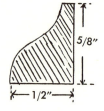

5/8"

1/2"

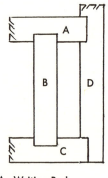

A—Writing Bed
B—Divider Between
   Drawer and Support
C—Base Frame
D—Side Panel

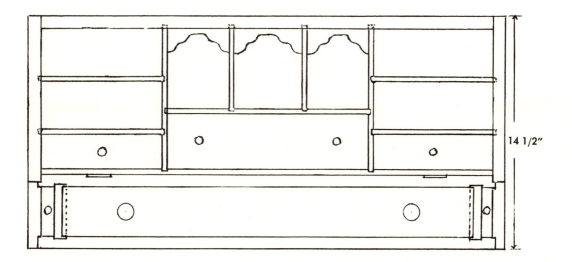

14 1/2"

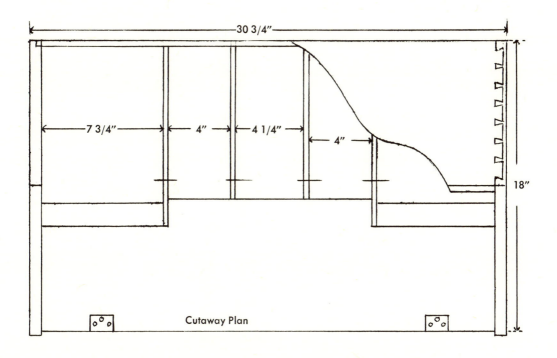

30 3/4"

7 3/4" 4" 4 1/4" 4"

18"

Cutaway Plan

Inches 0 1 2 3 4 5 6 7 8 9 10 11 12

from bottom edge. From now on, the side panels will be a pair—right and left. To prevent errors, use a square to draw pencil lines the width and position of the next series of cuts, also how far the grooves will go from back toward the front on both left and right panels. Make frequent checks with cross section at center.

Immediately above the writing bed groove there will be a 5/16″ panel to raise the drawers above the bed surface; this panel requires no side grooves but mark a line for it to keep measurements in order. The line ends from back to front 11 1/2″. Measure up from bed groove 2 5/16″ and 2 9/16″; square these lines in to 11 1/2″. Measure up from bed groove 6″ and 6 1/4″; square these lines in to 10 1/4″.

Mount the dado side cutters on arbor to cut 1/4″ grooves; raise cutters to 3/16″ height; set fence to cut the first grooves 2 5/16″ up, the second setting 6″ up. Do not cut past the stop marks. Square out the groove ends with a narrow chisel.

To be assured of a square case when completed, the lengths of top board, writing bed, and base frame are critical. The drawing calls for an overall width of 30 3/4″; subtracting 1 1/2″ for side panels, and adding 1/4″ for depth of bed and frame grooves, we end up with a figure of 29 1/2″; these two components are the same length. When determining the top board length, start with the inside of panels measurement which is 29 1/4″; this will be the distance between shoulders to be cut on the underside of top board. Add to this figure, 1/2″ on each end for 1/2″ × 1/2″ dovetails. Square-cut the top board to exactly 30 1/4″ long by 9 1/2″ wide. Make the base frame by sawing the front and back pieces 1 1/2″ × 3/4″ × 29 1/2″ long, the sides, 2″ × 3/4″ × 15 3/4″. If you are curious about the side piece length, start figuring backwards.

Set up the dado cutters with a 1/4″ spacer between; raise to cut 1/2″ plus high. Adjust the fence to place the 1/4″ tenon close to the center of 3/4″ wood; mark one side of all four frame pieces. Up-end a side piece, marked surface against the fence; pass over dado; repeat. Remove spacer to cut 1/4″ grooves; raise cutters slightly above previous setting. Set fence to place grooves exactly in line with the tenons, marked surface against fence; make groove cuts. Replace saw blade; set fence 1/2″ to the outside of blade; adjust height for tenon waste wood cut-off. Bore three 11/64″ screw holes through the width of side pieces (cross section at center).

Coat with glue the grooves in both front and back pieces; glue tenons; assemble by hand; place in two bar clamps; try square and, if necessary, angle the clamps to bring the frame into square. After setting, sand all joints flush. Before attaching to the side panel, be sure there is no hardened glue on the end edges squeezed out when assembling. Rough-sand writing bed top and bottom; finish-sand top surface. Set up the 3/4″ dado for grooves to align and position divider "B" on drawing. Raise cutters to 1/8″; set fence 1/8″ and 3/4″ to the near side of cutters; run these grooves from front to back on the underside of bed and upper surface of base frame.

The top board must have four 1/4″ grooves cut almost to the front edge (cutaway plan). Set up the dado side cutters; raise to 3/16″; set fence to 7 3/4″ plus 1/2″ for dovetails, 8 1/4″ to the near side of cutters, make cut from both ends; reset fence to 12 1/2″ for final cuts. These grooves run from back to front 8 1/2″; square out end of grooves with narrow chisel. Rabbet out the back under edge of top panel for plywood back, 5/16″ for the plywood thickness and 3/8″ toward the top surface, the same cuts to be made on side panels. Shoulders must be cut on the underside of top board to leave a protrusion 1/2″ on the top surface and 1/2″ from top down.

Before laying off for dovetails, the side panels must have the front corner cut on a slope. Observe carefully the top ending of slope and the point at the writing bed; space must be provided to fill the 7/16″ deep rabbet that will be cut on the writing leaf. This is accomplished by drawing a straight line from a point 9 1/4″ from back to front on the top edge of side panel and another point 9/16″ above the writing bed. Carefully band-saw to this line. Small blocks are glued to the side panels at the writing bed area to carry around the radius tracked by the leaf when being opened or closed (see cross section at center). For dovetailing, study the cutaway plan. It will be noted that the side panel can be viewed as the end of a drawer front with the top board being treated as a 1/2″ thick drawer side; cut these dovetails by following instructions in chapter on dovetailing. One other milling job before final sanding: The front edge of top board must have an approximate 45° angle cut on both the upper and lower corners (see cross section at center); this may be done on the jointer with fence set at 45°. Finish-sand the inside surfaces of side panels and the underside of top board.

Procedure for assembling is as follows: lay one side panel on the work table; place the base frame in bottom groove (keep the divider grooves up); sink three 2 1/2″ #8 screws through frame into side panel. Some help in assembling would make the job much easier. Lay the other side on table; now coat with glue both writing bed grooves; position the writing bed in the unattached frame side panel; turn over the side with frame fastened to it; position groove on writing bed end; align frame in groove; sink screws. Turn assembly upright; coat dovetails with glue; align top board and, using a block of wood to prevent marking, seat firmly in place with a heavy hammer.

If it is necessary, glue together 5/16″ and 1/4″ wood to get the sizes needed for the case interior; do it at this time. Start interior work with the 5/16″ base board; the drawing calls for it to be 11 1/2″ wide by the exact distance between side panels. As shown on cutaway, the center area of this board is cut to recess the center drawer. The cutout sets back 1 3/4″ and is 13″ wide, but this 13″ must match the distance between the outside grooves milled in the top board. If there is any difference, adjust the cutout to match. Run two 1/4″ grooves from front to back on the bottom board the exact distance from the side panels as those milled on the underside of top. Sand the front edge of this piece; place in position; nail down with about 4 one-inch head nails.

The end dividers are to be made next. Measure exactly the distance between the bottom surface of top and bottom grooves—this will be the length of dividers; square-cut to length; from the back edge mark the length of the top groove on the top edge of divider; the bottom comes flush with the bottom board 11 1/2". Use the 1/2" square block (detail on drawing) to mark the front edge for band-sawing. Fit these dividers into their slots and measure accurately the distance up to the first groove on a side panel—this should be 2". Mark dividers for matching 1/4" × 1/8" deep grooves to complete true rectangles. On the same divider sides, mark the exact distance to the upper shelf grooves as measured on a side panel; cut grooves.

On the other side of these dividers, measure up for grooves to leave an opening 3 1/2" high for the center drawer—these grooves end, from back to front 9 1/2". Square out groove ends; cut grooves; finish-sand curved front edges and all sides; spot the grooves, in a few places, with glue; slide into position both dividers. Cut and fit the panel that forms the cover for the center drawer; it should be 9 1/2" wide by about 13 1/4" long. On the top surface of this panel, run grooves from front to back and 4" in from the ends for pigeon holes. To be sure of vertical positioning, check the distance accurately from divider to groove in top board; match grooves in cover panel; sand front edge and top surface; spot-glue grooves and slide panel into place.

Measure, cut, and fit panels for covering end drawer openings and shelves; the covers should be 11 1/2" wide and the shelves 10". Finish-sand the front edges and top surfaces of covers—both top and bottom surfaces of shelves; spot-glue grooves; slide into place. Cut and fit two pigeon hole dividers—top 8 1/2" wide, bottom 9 1/2". Copy curve from 1/2" squared blocks; finish-sand front edges and all side surfaces. Spot-glue grooves; slide in place. The pigeon hole valances can be shaped to any curves that strike your fancy. They should be made of one piece about 1 1/4" high by 3/8" thick by a close fit in each opening; band-saw, sand, and glue the top edge; press in place.

Measure the height for a piece to fit in the grooves to divide and align the drawer and leaf support slides—they should be about 3 1/4" long by 3/4" thick by about 1 1/2" wide (width is unimportant). Fit a strip in each groove to continue the remaining distance to the back, these pieces to be 3/4" thick by about 1 1/2" high; coat grooves with glue; press strips into place. Make the slides to fit the openings—3" high by 17 1/2" long. Hand-plane for smooth sliding fit. Round all four right-angle edges to match the rounded drawer lips. Finish-sand all surfaces; place slides in slots; position them to let the rounded fronts protrude 1/4" from case front; glue and nail stop blocks on the case sides in back of slides.

The leaf will be a glued-up 3/4" thick panel 13 1/4" wide × 27 1/4"

rough length; after glue setting, square ends to a finish length of 26 1/4";
saw two battens for the ends 2" × 3/4" × 14 1/4" long; mark one side
of panel and one side of each batten. Set up dado side cutters with a
1/4" spacer between; raise to 1/2" plus; set fence to place tenon in center
of 3/4" wood; up-end panel; hold marked side against fence; pass over
dado; repeat. Remove spacer; raise cutters slightly above previous setting;
set fence to line up the groove with tenon; hold marked side of batten
against fence; pass over cutters; repeat. Replace dado with saw blade; set
fence to cut 1/2" waste wood from tenon shoulder; raise blade to cut
only the waste wood; repeat both sides of each panel end.

Coat batten grooves with glue; coat also the panel tenons. Start the
assembly by hand. Be sure to have batten wood protruding over each panel
edge; lay on two bar clamps and draw tight. After setting, cut off the
waste batten wood in line with panel edges—a light jointer cut will leave
a continuous straight smooth edge. Rough-sand both sides. Check measurements to see if the proposed rabbet cut of 7/16" deep (from inside surface toward lipped outside surface) by 1/4" wide on two side edges and
the top edge will leave at least 1/16" clearance on the three edges when
bottom inside corner meets the top corner of writing bed. In case of insufficient clearance, widen the 1/4" cut as much as is necessary.

As shown on the cutaway plan, rout out for two 1 1/2" butt hinges;
set router depth to the center of hinge pin; place a hinge on the bed,
lining up the pin with the bed ledge 3" in from case side; hold tight and outline with a scriber; repeat other end. Rout out close to the lines; clean
out with hand tools; fasten hinges with 1/2" brass screws of a number
to fit the holes. Pull out slides, place leaf on supports in its proper position, being sure to have equal clearance on each side. Outline hinges with
scriber; rout out and clean with hand tools. Fasten this side of hinges with
screws; close leaf to try fit; if it should bind any place, more wood can
be removed in that area with a bullnose plane.

The style drawer lock available for the leaf will have a back plate which
must be set into the wood flush with the surface. A router bit setting will
do this job quickly. Clean corners with hand tools; study the lock to see
where and how deep other cuts are required. The selvage must also be
set in flush with wood surface. A small brass strike plate will probably
have to be made; this is nothing more than a strip of brass with a slot
large enough to accommodate the lock bolt and a countersunk screw hole
on each end. This plate will be set into the lower 45° angle of the top
front edge. Check to see if the lip binds anywhere on the circle segment
as the leaf is opened or closed; if so, some wood must be removed from
case side to give necessary clearance. Also it may be necessary to remove
some wood on one or the other case side slope to allow the leaf to fit
down evenly all around. After those adjustments, finish-sand case edges;
remove leaf and hinges; round all four right-angle outside corners with
a hand plane; finish-sand all surfaces; be sure to remove all cross sand
scratches from battens.

If necessary, hand-plane the top surface in the dovetail area to smooth it out for sanding. Where no sanding has been done on the outside case surfaces, rough-sand, then fine-sand the entire case outside.

We will return to the frame for a moment to correct an omission: When the desk is placed on the frame, a border of 5/8" should show on the two sides and front. The front is no problem because the desk is resting on a 1 5/8" strip but the sides have only 3/4" in width. It will be well to screw to the side skirts strips to fit between the legs about 3/4" square. Fasten one also along the back skirt so a back screw as well as a front one will hold the desk on frame. Sink these attachment screws to prevent the desk from moving on the frame when nailing the division molding.

Division molding may be any shape your equipment can provide. Keep it to a height of 5/8" and width of 9/16", or 1/16" less than the ledge on top of frame. Miter both ends of front piece first; brad with one-inch #18 brads; miter side pieces; cut to length; brad in place.

All drawer fronts are of 5/8" thick wood; the frame drawer will have a lip on the top and two sides; the long drawer under the writing bed has two side lips but none on top because that would extend above the leaf support line; these large drawers have side, back, and bottom wood 3/8" thick; the three inside drawers use 1/4" thick for sides, backs, and bottoms. Size the lipped drawer fronts 1/2" longer than the opening and, in the case of frame drawer, 1/4" higher. The desk drawer has no top lip.

The two large drawers do not need stop blocks because the lips prevent them from moving into the case too far. Cut the interior drawer sides 1/2" short of the back line; this leaves space to glue and nail a small block on each side wall. Fit the lipped drawer fronts as well as the small ones into their openings and provide at least 1/16" play. Follow normal drawer dovetailing as explained in Chapter 2.

Cut the 1/4" plywood to fit the back space. It is suggested that this piece be left separate until finishing is completed.

THE STAIN MIX FOR PINE IS

3/4 Light oak
1/8 Danish walnut
1/8 American cherry

APPENDIX

It may not occur to the reader that with almost every piece of furniture illustrated some details can be varied, if so desired. It is even more important to realize that sizes (except for the Plank Bottom Chair) can range over a wide latitude without altering the basic construction procedure. In every case of a size change, transpose the affected measurements and proceed according to text and drawing.

Where drawers are involved, keep the openings close to the scale of overall change, then make the drawers to fit. All size change is simply a matter of recomputing measurements, not altering structural instructions.

It is possible that the maker may find it desirable to change the size but not the shape of the Cove Cupboard to fit a projected area; just change measurements.

A piece that can be changed widely in shape and size is the Dining Table. Instead of a round, possibly an oval would be interesting? A large square? A rectangle, varying in length and width to suit the need? All of these suggestions still retain the basic parts, ie. four unchanged legs, four unchanged skirts, except for length, and the same 1 1/8" top boards.

The Trestle Table may be changed to twice the size without design change. Larger than that it would be necessary to increase wood thickness to 1 1/8".

The suggested use of a portable router or sander has been deliberately omitted. Unless one has experience in their use, considerable risk is involved. On the other hand, sanding large flat surfaces by hand is extremely discouraging. If a power sander is used, it should be a 3" or 4" belt machine. Orbital or oscillating types require considerable handsanding with the grain to erase the circular scratches left by the machine.

Also available from
STEIN AND DAY

**FINE FURNITURE FOR
THE AMATEUR CABINETMAKER**
by A.W. Marlow

CLASSIC FURNITURE PROJECTS
by A.W. Marlow

HOW TO BUILD PERIOD COUNTRY FURNITURE
by V. J. Taylor

**PRACTICAL UPHOLSTERING
AND THE CUTTING OF SLIP COVERS**
by Frederick Palmer

THE COMPLETE DICTIONARY OF WOOD
by Thomas Corkhill

THE COMPLETE MANUAL OF WOOD FINISHING
by Frederick Oughton

HOW TO PAINT ANYTHING
The Complete Guide to Painting and Refinishing
by Hubbard H. Cobb

DO-IT-YOURSELF HOUSEBUILDING
Step-By-Step
by Charles D. Neal

CHAMPAGNE DECORATING ON A BEER BUDGET
by Doreen Roy

THE COMPLETE MOBILE HOME BOOK
The Guide to Manufactured Homes
by Nicholas Raskhodoff

OUTDOOR POWER EQUIPMENT
How It Works, How to Fix It
by Arthur Darack